THE FUTURE OF FARMING: TECHNOLOGICAL INNOVATIONS, OPPORTUNITIES, AND CHALLENGES FOR PRODUCERS

HEARING

BEFORE THE

SUBCOMMITTEE ON
GENERAL FARM COMMODITIES
AND RISK MANAGEMENT

OF THE

COMMITTEE ON AGRICULTURE
HOUSE OF REPRESENTATIVES

ONE HUNDRED FIFTEENTH CONGRESS

FIRST SESSION

JULY 13, 2017

Serial No. 115–9

Printed for the use of the Committee on Agriculture
agriculture.house.gov

U.S. GOVERNMENT PUBLISHING OFFICE
26–385 PDF WASHINGTON : 2017

For sale by the Superintendent of Documents, U.S. Government Publishing Office
Internet: bookstore.gpo.gov Phone: toll free (866) 512–1800; DC area (202) 512–1800
Fax: (202) 512–2104 Mail: Stop IDCC, Washington, DC 20402–0001

COMMITTEE ON AGRICULTURE

K. MICHAEL CONAWAY, Texas, *Chairman*

GLENN THOMPSON, Pennsylvania
  Vice Chairman
BOB GOODLATTE, Virginia,
FRANK D. LUCAS, Oklahoma
STEVE KING, Iowa
MIKE ROGERS, Alabama
BOB GIBBS, Ohio
AUSTIN SCOTT, Georgia
ERIC A. "RICK" CRAWFORD, Arkansas
SCOTT DesJARLAIS, Tennessee
VICKY HARTZLER, Missouri
JEFF DENHAM, California
DOUG LaMALFA, California
RODNEY DAVIS, Illinois
TED S. YOHO, Florida
RICK W. ALLEN, Georgia
MIKE BOST, Illinois
DAVID ROUZER, North Carolina
RALPH LEE ABRAHAM, Louisiana
TRENT KELLY, Mississippi
JAMES COMER, Kentucky
ROGER W. MARSHALL, Kansas
DON BACON, Nebraska
JOHN J. FASO, New York
NEAL P. DUNN, Florida
JODEY C. ARRINGTON, Texas

COLLIN C. PETERSON, Minnesota, *Ranking Minority Member*
DAVID SCOTT, Georgia
JIM COSTA, California
TIMOTHY J. WALZ, Minnesota
MARCIA L. FUDGE, Ohio
JAMES P. McGOVERN, Massachusetts
FILEMON VELA, Texas, *Vice Ranking Minority Member*
MICHELLE LUJAN GRISHAM, New Mexico
ANN M. KUSTER, New Hampshire
RICHARD M. NOLAN, Minnesota
CHERI BUSTOS, Illinois
SEAN PATRICK MALONEY, New York
STACEY E. PLASKETT, Virgin Islands
ALMA S. ADAMS, North Carolina
DWIGHT EVANS, Pennsylvania
AL LAWSON, JR., Florida
TOM O'HALLERAN, Arizona
JIMMY PANETTA, California
DARREN SOTO, Florida
LISA BLUNT ROCHESTER, Delaware

MATTHEW S. SCHERTZ, *Staff Director*
ANNE SIMMONS, *Minority Staff Director*

SUBCOMMITTEE ON GENERAL FARM COMMODITIES AND RISK MANAGEMENT

ERIC A. "RICK" CRAWFORD, Arkansas, *Chairman*

FRANK D. LUCAS, Oklahoma
MIKE ROGERS, Alabama
BOB GIBBS, Ohio
AUSTIN SCOTT, Georgia
SCOTT DesJARLAIS, Tennessee
RICK W. ALLEN, Georgia
MIKE BOST, Illinois
RALPH LEE ABRAHAM, Louisiana
DON BACON, Nebraska
NEAL P. DUNN, Florida
JODEY C. ARRINGTON, Texas

RICHARD M. NOLAN, Minnesota, *Ranking Minority Member*
TIMOTHY J. WALZ, Minnesota
CHERI BUSTOS, Illinois
LISA BLUNT ROCHESTER, Delaware
DAVID SCOTT, Georgia
SEAN PATRICK MALONEY, New York
STACEY E. PLASKETT, Virgin Islands
AL LAWSON, JR., Florida
TOM O'HALLERAN, Arizona

CONTENTS

	Page
Crawford, Hon. Eric A. "Rick", a Representative in Congress from Arkansas, opening statement	1
Prepared statement	2
Nolan, Hon. Richard M., a Representative in Congress from Minnesota, opening statement	3

WITNESSES

Tiller, Billy, Co-Founder and Advisor to the CEO, Grower Information Services Cooperative, Lubbock, TX	5
Prepared statement	7
Janzen, J.D., Todd J., President, Janzen Agricultural Law LLC, Indianapolis, IN	18
Prepared statement	19
Casurella, Deborah, Chief Executive Officer, Independent Data Management, LLC, Hudson, WI	28
Prepared statement	29
Royse, J.D., Roger, Founder and Owner, Royse Law Firm, PC and Royse AgTech Innovation Network, Menlo Park, CA	35
Prepared statement	36

(III)

THE FUTURE OF FARMING: TECHNOLOGICAL INNOVATIONS, OPPORTUNITIES, AND CHALLENGES FOR PRODUCERS

THURSDAY, JULY 13, 2017

House of Representatives,
Subcommittee on General Farm Commodities and Risk Management,
Committee on Agriculture,
Washington, D.C.

The Subcommittee met, pursuant to call, at 10:01 a.m., in Room 1300, Longworth House Office Building, Hon. Eric A. "Rick" Crawford [Chairman of the Subcommittee] presiding.

Members present: Representatives Crawford, Gibbs, Allen, Abraham, Bacon, Dunn, Arrington, Nolan, Walz, Bustos, Blunt Rochester, Maloney, Plaskett, Lawson, and O'Halleran.

Staff present: Emily Wong, Mollie Wilken, Rachel Millard, Trevor White, Liz Friedlander, Mike Stranz, Troy Phillips, Nicole Scott, and Carly Reedholm.

OPENING STATEMENT OF HON. ERIC A. "RICK" CRAWFORD, A REPRESENTATIVE IN CONGRESS FROM ARKANSAS

The CHAIRMAN. Good morning. This hearing of the Subcommittee on General Farm Commodities and Risk Management entitled, *The Future of Farming: Technological Innovations, Opportunities, and Challenges for Producers,* will come to order. Thank you for joining us today.

Yesterday, the full Committee held a productive discussion on how technology is influencing specialty crop production. Today, our Subcommittee will explore how promising new information technologies, and the increasing utilization of data in agriculture, are influencing the future of farming.

It is a critical time for everyone involved in production agriculture as we face tough choices ahead. Given tight margins and a continued slump in the prices at the farm gate, even routine day-to-day decision making can determine whether the farmer will turn an annual profit. These challenges in farm country underscore the importance of the decisions we make in the next farm bill, which we will have to write with fewer resources than we had the last go-round.

But as we begin to answer the tough questions, one thing is clear for farmers and policymakers alike: Technology plays an undeniably important role in how we address these challenges. The decisions we make surrounding data and agriculture technology will decide the future of farming in America and impact producers for years to come as technologies continue to expand and evolve.

This is the third hearing we have held in the last year-and-a-half related to big data and the ground is already quickly shifting. Big data is influencing planting decisions, optimizing yields, it gives farmers tools to more accurately assess soil health and water usage, and it is even cutting down on labor costs. Farmers are also quickly learning that smart investments in new technology will not only make them more efficient, but will also conserve resources and ensure their land will remain productive for generations to come. Finally, big data is making USDA farm programs more accurate, efficient, and easier for farmers to navigate.

But while cutting-edge technology promises many benefits, there are also significant challenges to overcome. There continues to be considerable uncertainty in the legal and regulatory landscape. Farmers are justifiably concerned about the privacy and security of their data, while questions loom over data ownership. Inadequate rural broadband access is also a significant barrier for farmers who lack the high-speed Internet needed to take full advantage of the innovations we are discussing today. And, as the industry continues to make investments in its future, the Federal Government must keep pace to modernize and adapt to a rapidly changing environment.

Our distinguished witnesses here with us today will present some of the promising benefits of big data in agriculture and will also enlighten us about how they are tackling the many challenges they are facing. I look forward to hearing their views as we assess the role of government in the modernization of agriculture. I believe this is key to ensuring that America remains the most abundant and affordable supplier of food and fiber in the world.

[The prepared statement of Mr. Crawford follows:]

PREPARED STATEMENT OF HON. ERIC A. "RICK" CRAWFORD, A REPRESENTATIVE IN CONGRESS FROM ARKANSAS

Thank you for joining us today.

Yesterday, the full Committee held a productive discussion on how technology is influencing specialty crop production. Today, our Subcommittee will explore how promising new information technologies and the increasing utilization of data in agriculture is influencing the future of farming.

It is a critical time for everyone involved in production agriculture as we face tough choices ahead. Given tight margins and a continued slump in prices at the farm gate, even routine, day-to-day decision-making can determine whether the farmer will turn an annual profit. These challenges in farm country underscore the importance of the decisions we make in the next farm bill, which we will have to write with fewer resources than we had the last go-round.

But as we begin to answer the tough questions, one thing's clear—for farmers and policymakers alike—technology plays an undeniably important role in how we address these challenges. The decisions we make surrounding data and agriculture technology will decide the future of farming in America and impact producers for years to come as technologies continue expanding and evolving.

This is the third hearing we've held in the last year-and-a-half related to big data and the ground is already quickly shifting. Big data is influencing planting decisions and optimizing yields, it gives farmers tools to more accurately assess soil health and water usage, and it's even cutting down on labor costs. Farmers are also quickly learning that smart investments in new technology will not only make them more efficient, but will also conserve resources and ensure their land will remain productive for generations to come. Finally, big data is making USDA farm programs more accurate, efficient and easier for farmers to navigate.

But while cutting-edge agriculture technology promises many benefits, there are also significant challenges to overcome. There continues to be considerable uncertainty in the legal and regulatory landscape. Farmers are justifiably concerned about the privacy and security of their data while questions loom over data ownership. Inadequate rural broadband access is also a significant barrier for many farmers who lack the high-speed Internet needed to take full advantage of the innovations we are discussing today. And, as the industry continues making investments in its future, the Federal Government must keep pace to modernize and adapt to a rapidly changing environment.

Our distinguished witnesses here with us today will present some of the promising benefits of big data in agriculture, and will also enlighten us about how they are tackling the many challenges they're facing. I look forward to hearing their views as we assess the role of government in the modernization of agriculture. I believe this is key to ensuring that America remains the most abundant and affordable supplier of food and fiber in the world.

The CHAIRMAN. I would now like to recognize my friend, the Ranking Member from Minnesota, Mr. Nolan, for any comments he would like to make.

OPENING STATEMENT OF HON. RICHARD M. NOLAN, A REPRESENTATIVE IN CONGRESS FROM MINNESOTA

Mr. NOLAN. Can you hear me? There we go. I had it covered up.

Thank you, Chairman Crawford, for getting me turned on here, if you will pardon the expression. But I thank the other Members of the Committee, the Subcommittee here, for holding this important hearing regarding the future of farming and the opportunities and the challenges presented by data technology innovations.

And thanks to the great panel of witnesses that we have here. We thank you for coming. We have a couple old sayings around this town. First is, you better come to town and make a case for yourself, because if you don't there is a possibility that this town might not know you exist. Worse yet, if they know you exist and you don't show up, they might think you don't care. Thank you for taking the time to be here.

And you should know that the proceedings and the knowledge and the information garnered here will end up going far beyond the Members of this Committee and our staffs. It is reviewed and paid attention to by policymakers and thinkers and advocates not just in this country, but all over the world. Your testimony is very, very important here today.

And the other old admonition is that in this town, if you are not at the table you might be on the menu, and you don't want to be there.

So welcome.

The fact is that technology innovations have greatly benefited our farm economy. My gosh, when I was first elected to the Congress, if you reaped 80, 90 bushels an acre of corn, you were an all-star. And nowadays, why, it is like get out of town, where have you been? We have quadrupled yields, not just for corn but so many of the other important commodities that have not only helped feed America, but have helped feed in many cases a starving and a hungry world. Agriculture has played such an incredibly important role in our economy and in the world economy.

More recently, farmers have become more efficient with those crop yields, as I mentioned, do a better job of predicting the environment and innovation there through the use of data technologies. And while we have undoubtedly seen great benefits from these innovations, there are also important questions we must answer related to ownership of data collected on farms as well as its security and its privacy.

We must also assure that access to information is balanced, does not allow for the manipulation of markets, as we have sometimes seen in the past. Some of us may remember how clever the Russians were back in the seventies at manipulating our farm markets, not to imply any parallels with what is happening today.

Finally, we must continue to invest in rural America, broadband, to ensure that our producers have the ability to receive and to send data at acceptable speeds and affordable prices.

High-speed broadband is not unlike what the REA and the Rural Telephone Administration were for past generations. If you don't have the latest communications capabilities, you are out of luck. You are not going to grow. You are not going to prosper. You are not going to be able to fully communicate and participate in all that America has to offer.

American agriculture might be entering a new era because of these data technologies, but we need to make sure farmers and rural communities benefit from these innovations as well.

So with that said, I am looking forward to your testimony. I know all the other Members of the Subcommittee are looking forward to your testimony as well. And once again, I thank Chairman Crawford for holding this important hearing.

Mr. Chairman, I yield the balance of my time.

The CHAIRMAN. Thank you, sir, I appreciate it.

We have four distinguished witnesses with us here today, and I want to introduce each one of them. But first I would like to recognize the gentleman from Texas to introduce our first witness.

Mr. Arrington, cotton-eyed Jodey, you are recognized.

Mr. ARRINGTON. There is a story to that, but I will spare you. Thank you, Mr. Chairman. It is my honor to introduce to you a fellow west Texan and a friend from my hometown of Lubbock, Texas, Billy Tiller. He is a fourth-generation ag producer. He received his accounting degree from the greatest university in the land, Texas Tech University. He has been on a bank board. And as a CPA, he understands the business of agriculture, and he certainly has a unique perspective on industry profitability and those challenges as an ag lender and what they present to our ag lenders.

He is an entrepreneur and he has been involved in ag technology startup companies, where I met him as Vice Chancellor for Research and Technology Commercialization at Texas Tech. He and his wife Crystal are parents of four children and five grandchildren.

We got to visit before this hearing, and I said, "What do you want me to say about your background?" He said, "Two things: I am a cotton farmer." And that is what he is most proud to be known as, is a cotton farmer. He said, "If you are going to do something to help the cotton farmers, I am in. If you are not, I am not going to be a part of it."

That is my philosophy too, Billy. Thank you for being here.

And, Mr. Chairman, thank you for indulging me.

The CHAIRMAN. Yes, sir, thank you. The gentleman yields back.

I would like to introduce Mr. Todd Janzen, President, Janzen Agricultural Law, from Indianapolis, Indiana.

Welcome.

Ms. Deb Casurella, CEO, Independent Data Management, Hudson, Wisconsin. And finally, Mr. Roger Royse, founder of Royse Law Firm in Menlo Park, California.

I would like to direct the witnesses, direct your attention to the lights in front of you, a green light, a yellow light, and a red light. It is just like driving. When you see the light is green, keep your foot on the gas; when it turns yellow, get ready to stop; and when it is red, slam on the brakes. And we will get through this and get to our questions as quickly as we can.

So, having said that, I would like to recognize our first witness. Mr. Billy Tiller, you are recognized for 5 minutes.

STATEMENT OF BILLY TILLER, CO-FOUNDER AND ADVISOR TO THE CEO, GROWER INFORMATION SERVICES COOPERATIVE, LUBBOCK, TX

Mr. TILLER. Thank you, Chairman Crawford, Ranking Member Nolan. And Jodey, thank you for the introduction.

I would like to add something to his introduction. In the data world, I am about all farmers. And the beauty is we all collect acres, we all have planting varieties, and we have seed, and we put out chemicals. As we do all these things, it is all measured against land. If I do it in cotton, you can do it in corn, you can do it in soybeans, you can do it in specialty crops. That is the beauty of what is going on.

He has pretty well introduced me, so I am going to jump right into what is going on here. I have a grower information services cooperative that I founded. It is a cooperative owned by growers. The idea behind it was to create value and control for the grower.

Because what we are dealing with today is really a world where there is some fear among growers, what is going on in this data world. If we have a governing board at the cooperative, I am hoping this continues to grow, I think you will see that really taking hold.

We have 41 states covered, about 1,400 members. And out of that, I would say there are 10,000 growers that have talked to me in the last 5 years, have tremendous interest. And when the platform is up and fully functional, you will see those growers come in to help us.

I want to talk today about the opportunities, the challenges, and literally the innovations in agriculture. I could focus on GiSC, but I want to talk about what I have been able to see in the last few years.

And as I say that, the opportunity is real. Ag 2.0 and Ag 3.0 is here, and we are seeing some things happen now around the Internet of Things. There are a lot of challenges to creating adoption in agriculture, and they are due to the fact that I have had a lot of tools created for me and many of them I don't need. They don't solve any of my pain points. They look cool, they cost a lot of money, but I am looking for things I can actually put into the farm, I can implement, and that I can use to collect data.

I would say that so far the value has not exceeded the maximum cost that has been charged for some of these things, not all them, but a lot of them. I think there is also fear on the part of the grower not understanding what is going on. You will be interested in Mr. Janzen's testimony about something called the Transparency Evaluator that is very vital to the industry.

The other thing I would say are the time factors. Farmers are caught up in prioritizing and reprioritizing their time on daily basis. When they are collecting data it has to be more of an automated fashion. It has to be autonomous. They are not going to go in at night and spend 3 hours actually entering data about seed varieties and those sorts of things. They are through at the end of the day. We will be able to use new technologies that you see coming onto the forefront to be able to automatically or semiautomatically collect data.

There has been a lot of ag hype, and it has been promises, promises, promises that have gone on around ag tech companies and hundreds of millions of dollars that have been invested, and yet they haven't solved our problem. Money hasn't quite been the issue.

The ownership issue is there. I would love to sit with any of you and talk about that. But the ownership of the data, it is a critical issue. I have groups today tell me, "Billy, your co-op, your members, you can't own your data." I mean, that is ludicrous to me. What do you mean, I can't own my data? Are you going to go tell a small business owner he can't own his data? That is the craziest thing I have ever heard. Just because I use a certain piece of equipment, I can't own the data?

I am hung up on I am going to own my data off my cotton farm, and that way I can do things with it. And I may share it with third parties so I can get value.

Then there is the concern about disruption in the industry. There is no doubt we have disruption going on in the industry, and that creates fear among the industry players. We have to literally stop the fear among the industry players so they feel like that we can move forward.

I want to hit a few points before I run out of time here, and those are, how could you help us? One problem we have is we need to make sure that we have the rural broadband, the connectivity in place, and that is a place this Committee could really play.

I am going to ask you to really think hard as you are making those investments into the USF fund, those sorts of things. We have to have them, because we need speed.

I am going to tell you, if these millennials want their food to talk, and they do, they want traceability, the only way we are going to make it talk is to actually have connectivity all the way back to the field level. Keep that in mind.

People are moving to town, but the land is never going to move, so we need the connectivity back. It is not so much for the residents. It will help, telemedicine, all those things, but it is so that we can use it on the farms.

I want to wrap up by talking about on the challenges something Ken Zuckerberg said. Ken is the head of research for Rabobank, and in a statement he said: "We believe that a standardized system is necessary to drive farmer adoption of digital agriculture services. Yet without a common data platform and operating system, it is unlikely that growers, or the vendors providing precision farming services, will fully capture the value associated with digital agriculture."

I would say this last: We are working with a lot of companies, from big ones like IDM and The Weather Company, great things that we can innovate and bring right in to groups like Farmobile and their PUC, to groups like IBM, and Deb's reporting tool that you are going to hear about. These things are there. We just have to integrate them, get them back to the farmer.

Thank you for what you do for the American farmer. I am so appreciative of how you all build and create and protect the CLU layer and all those things that you do around section 6 and section 1619. Thank you for your hard work.

[The prepared statement of Mr. Tiller follows:]

PREPARED STATEMENT OF BILLY TILLER, CO-FOUNDER AND ADVISOR TO THE CEO, GROWER INFORMATION SERVICES COOPERATIVE, LUBBOCK, TX

Good morning. My name is Billy Tiller, founder of Grower Information Services Cooperative (GiSC). I am honored to be given the opportunity to talk to you about the state of ag data innovation today. My interests in this subject are personal; not only as the founder of GiSC, but also as a 4th generation farmer operating a 6,400 acre family farm in the high plains of west Texas, producing cotton, grain sorghum, and sunflowers. As a farmer who has long realized the value of digital data systems—from the efficiencies of digital information capture and data exchange to the productivity potential of data analysis—I began to see the almost endless use cases for technology applications for my operation and my partners' operations in the food & fiber supply chain. In 2010, I began a conversation with my longtime friend and associate Monty Edwards, a large crop insurance agent with deep generational roots in agriculture, about how digital technologies could improve our businesses, communications with partners, and ultimately, our quality of life.

Through those conversations and additional investigation, we determined a unified, digital agri-information system with certain capabilities was needed to truly "digitally transform" farm operation information. Ideally, this information system would be capable of: (1) capturing and collecting significant farm operation data, (2) organizing and normalizing that data into logical data sets; and (3) sharing information, both from farmers to their trusted third parties and from those third parties back to farmers (with farmers in control of that sharing). At the time GiSC was formed in late 2012, the then commercially available technology existed to create an information system with these capabilities. However, at that time no such system, or similar solution, had been adopted by growers on any scale.

Today, in 2017, that continues to remain the case. Farmers' data related to their operations are stored in "data silos." Some of that data are stored in various "clouds", uploaded from technology applications purchased by fa[r]mers or provided to them by various vendors. Other data are stored locally in thumb drives and hard drives. Yet even more data are recorded on paper, stored on farmers' pickup truck dashboards and farm office desks and filing cabinets.

GiSC sprang from the conclusion that the "disconnect" between current information collection and distribution practices and the digital possibilities was (and continues to be) at least as much a business organizational problem as a technology problem and involves the relative value of farmers' data. Unlike the data captured and communicated on typical technology/information platforms for consumers, such as social media platforms, farm operation data is, in essence, intellectual property—the farmer's trade secrets and "know-how." Farmers are hesitant (and rightfully so) to entrust that data with third parties in which those farmers have no vested interest.

Bridging this disconnect, for us, was to turn to an organizational form U.S. growers have turned to for generations to solve shared problems: farmer cooperatives. Granted, the vision of GiSC, as a data cooperative, was a unique idea back in 2012 and, as far as I am aware, remains a one-of-a-kind organization to this day. GiSC, as a technology/business platform, provides its farmer-members what no other platform can: real control over their Intellectual Property, their farm operation data.

By offering a secure data platform service (an integrated system of technology tools and applications) to its members, GiSC can provide the obvious benefits of digitalization to an industry that finds itself outpaced by most other industries in information technology adoption, while at the same time protecting farmers' interest in their data. A cooperative is owned by its members. Farmers, by owning the service that provides the digital platform to capture, collect, and store operational data, are afforded two valuable and distinct advantages:

- Control—Through the data governance provided by GiSC (its members and board of directors) and GiSC's primary value proposition: growers own all the data that originates on their operations or from their operations' activities.
- Value—GiSC is uniquely positioned to return value back to its farmer-members for their willingness to include their data in the Coop's digital platform, whether in the form of operational benchmarks and insights, advanced data analytics, and/or member patronage.

GiSC Today: At a Glance

GiSC has grown from those initial conversations in 2010 and its formation in 2012 to a nation-wide cooperative, with 1,400 forward looking farmer-members from 41 states. GiSC has developed a vast network of loyal supporters who share its vision. As an example, GiSC has built a strong working relationship with the Agricultural Data Coalition (ADC), a coalition of research universities, prominent grower organizations and associations, equipment manufacturers, and regional input/service providers. These entities came together in an effort to help farmers better control and manage their data and to promote innovation in the industry. GiSC and ADC continue to work together to identify synergies and target opportunities for cooperation in areas in which the two organizations share mutually aligned values.

The fact is many things have changed for GiSC since its inception to today. However, GiSC's three key objectives, the Coop's cornerstone and foundation, remain the same.

(1) Bring attention to farmers' vested interest in their farm operation data and continue, with like-minded individuals and organizations, to establish the precedent that growers should (and must) own and control the data related to their agricultural operations.

(2) Offer its farmer-members (and future members) a secure digital platform that functions as a central repository for all of the grower's operational data, while providing governance of how that data is treated through the cooperative model.

(3) Return value back to its farmer-members as the digital platform grows in both users and information.

GiSC has faced a myriad of challenges raising the capital necessary to architect a robust digital platform, especially given the premise that ownership of that platform resides with its members. In spite of those challenges, GiSC stands on the precipice of bringing its vision to reality. GiSC is working with Ag Simplicity, LLC to integrate GiSC's licensed Authenticated Information Exchange platform with the information technology applications Ag Simplicity is currently developing. The integrated system, to be offered as AgSimp™ through GiSC to its members, provides key components for a robust, comprehensive digital platform solution. These components include:

- A simple on-farm data collection solution that provides real-time operational data capture with little effort or time from farm operators;
- A secure, cloud based Farm Information Management System with the capabilities to:
  » Interface with other technology tools and services utilized in a farm operation, collecting the data generated from those tools and services;
  » Synchronize all data sources for the most complete picture of an operation's activity; and
  » Organize growers' information geo-spatially, tagging information to its related farms/fields; [and]
- An agri-data exchange information and sharing platform that facilitates the Coop's farmer-members sharing data with trusted third parties, with member control over sharing capabilities.

The future vision for GiSC and the AgSimp™ platform solution is to provide additional value back to its members through data analysis as the wealth of information in the system grows.

The Future of Farming: The Opportunity of Digital Ag

From my experiences working with growers and industry leaders, I would say there is much evidence that the clear majority of farmers are not using data in any sort of systematic approach. This concept of utilizing farm data as a real operational toolset has been used in a million slide presentations to say that data-driven decision making is the next ag revolution, and Ag 2.0 (Ag Tech) heading to Ag 3.0 (Internet of Things) will feed the ever-growing world with less arable land. However, nobody has cracked this nut; the opportunity is the grandest of visions, but it has not been proven at any scale.

Ultimately, these circumstances should encourage us, not deter us, in the attempt to get a handle on this huge opportunity. Oh yes, the opportunity is real to utilize data to decrease costs and increase the efficiency of farming practices and make each field, the crop factory, perform to its potential, and we should view the current state of digital utilization on the farm as a blank slate: ripe for deploying the most powerful, yet cost effective, technologies available.

The Future of Farming: The Challenges of Digital Ag

Adoption Issues

I want to take these few moments to cover the topic that I know best: the practical use of agricultural technology in my operation under "in the field" conditions. As a farm operator, I am in the middle of the pack regarding ag technology adoption, putting me in a similar position to most U.S. farmers in the market today. I am always searching for morsels of value: actual uses of technology to solve real problems in my operation. This is tough investigative work when the industry is fixated on the buzzwords of "big data" and "game changing platforms". The truth is "you have to crawl before you walk." For all the "game changing platforms" flooding the market, there is not enough data captured in a useable format to create any real and usable analytics in the industry at any scale, much less the "big data" answers. I think this is shocking to most people that are not inside of the daily operations of a farm.

This is the dirty little secret in this data revolution: an actual shot has not been fired and the adoption of the current data solutions is at best defined as anemic. There has been a rash of "soft-adoption" in the past 2 years as Ag Tech start-ups offered farmers free chances to try the tools. Evidently however, farmers are for the most part not attracted to "cool tools" or the latest fad. They don't want any tool that takes more time to learn and use than the perceived value any such tool garners. The second part of the problem is the huge data gap from operating in equipment-centric solutions that capture data with equipment, yet doesn't interact effectively with the operator. The operator has many "points of light" in his little black book, and these data points are often not captured in equipment-centric solutions. For example, the seed variety and chemical cocktail used at planting may never be entered to the controller. My guess is the most widely planted variety of corn, as it is labeled in the controller, is just "CORN".

There are a multitude of reasons why this data is not entered into the controller. One of those reasons that should not be discounted is the concern over who else is able to use that data if the data are captured on a piece of equipment with telematics transferring that data directly into a vendor's cloud. Last, the real problem is that growers do not see the value in collecting this data, so they do not slow down to put the needed information it in the controller. This is a classic "the chicken or the egg" problem because the value comes from recommendations based on the analysis of good data. The data is not fully collected and most data sets have tremendous gaps in the necessary components to make them valuable without much post collection operations.

I have people say to me that it is impossible to have farmers purchase something they don't know they need. This is a challenge, but I am hopeful that we will see the adoption by growers. There are a couple anecdotes about Texas Instruments (TI) overcoming "adoption" challenges that I love. The first involved transistors. Pat Haggerty, then CEO of TI, realized that if he could create a radio small enough that it be carried on a person, these small radios would become a fad, developing a dynamic market for the transistor radio. He was right, but it was not just size: creating demand for the product meant getting the price point right too. A decade later Pat Haggerty challenged Jack Kilby, a TI lead engineer, to create a market for microchips by using them in "pocket" calculators. Pat wanted them small enough to fit in a shirt pocket and cheap enough to buy on impulse. The rest is history:

people, who had previously not realized they needed or wanted such a product, began to buy the calculators. Turns out, almost everyone had a need, and was willing to pay, for the convenience of on the spot addition, subtraction, multiplication, and division. These markets were born out of TI's innovative approach. Not only its approach to technological innovation, but also, and maybe more importantly, its marketing innovations.

We are at a similar place in the ag tech sector. There are obvious adoption challenges to overcome, but the answers are in sight. Solving the adoption dilemma is going to be defined by a product or set of products that solve *real* farm problems, especially problems which are either time consuming or expensive to solve today, and, much like the TI examples, the solutions must be packaged to attract grower's attention and their price points must be fair and reasonable in the grower's eyes. Second, as emphasized above, farm operation data is actually intellectual property and the grower must feel that the service provider has not overstepped in the use of the farmer's data nor violated his privacy rights. The challenges are daunting but I see a bright future for innovation that keeps in mind the value and the trust needed to handle the grower's data.

Time Factors

The challenges that make data collection in agriculture such a difficult task is just the nature of the process. Data collection, if it is done well, is a time-consuming task that must be carried out systematically, but farmers are under constantly changing pressures: prioritizing, and then re-prioritizing the work for the day. Farming is a highly time sensitive occupation. If you were to ask me what differentiates the most profitable farmers from the least profitable farmers, I would say the differentiator is not any one farmer's land, equipment, education, or even technology. The most critical element to thriving in a farming business is "timing".

Timing is everything, and it makes farming a race from start to finish. Timing in land preparation, seeding, fertilization placement, insecticide application, tillage, herbicide application, harvest, and marketing separates farmers into categories of failing, simply surviving, or thriving. Farming is a never-ending battle with the forces of nature and markets, and performing and making decision within these timing windows is difficult. External events outside the grower's control, such as weather, can at times humble the very best farm managers. This year, for me is just such an example: the cotton growing regions around Lubbock have been the most challenging in my 35 year career. Technology has helped me to compensate for the challenging year, but its benefits cannot overcome the forces beyond my control: hail, blowing sand, and other adverse conditions. However, it can help me analyze and diagnose my current situation and help me decide the most opportune direction to move to salvage the year.

The point is a farmer is deciding at any given moment what activity will make the biggest difference, when the year is over, to the bottom line. Effective data analysis from effective data collection will make a difference, but, for farmers, questions remain. Will it make as big a difference as getting this field harvested before an approaching storm system blows down my grain as it is ready to be harvested? Will it make a difference if the approaching rains "string out" my beautiful white field of cotton and lower the quality and then the price? These sort of situations is how gaps in data collection happen and this is one reason why farmers are not going to commit to time-consuming and costly processes, platforms, or services. We are looking for the "biggest bang for the buck" in both real dollars and time invested in the process.

However, I always am reminded of a recent statement of Jeremy Wilson, Technology Specialist at Crop IMS: "At the end of the day you only get one chance to collect data accurately and if you miss it when that machine goes through the field, you cannot get it back." Jeremy is a good friend and a great proponent of precision ag. I know he is right. I also know if we don't collect harvest data in 2017, then the next chance we will have to collect harvest data is another year away. A farmer is going to need to see the real, useable value that can be garnered from this collected data for him to slow down any and do the necessary data collection, accurately and in real-time.

Ag Tech Hype

One of the most significant challenges that is yet to be overcome by any single technology, or integrated technologies, in today's ag tech world is to create a product that: (1) solves a myriad of real pain points in agriculture, and (2) does so at a price point and time utilization metric that is attractive to growers. Both factors are needed to create value. Farmers are hopeful and are waiting, but the reality has not matched the hype. Technology companies, for the most part, have over promised what their "game changing platform" will do for the grower. Farmers, as a result, have become extremely skeptical about technology and how to incorporate it in their operations. I love a term used by Jason Tatge, CEO of Farmobile. He calls it "Ag-Tech Fatigue". Farmers have tried to see the value in the products offered, but the promises were over blown and using these products often became a leach on the grower's time. In many cases, even if the time consumed to use the product were not excessive, the actual cost of the product would be out of line with a farmer's expectation once the trial period was complete. Last, given the amount of time and money are acceptable, the grower may still be uncomfortable with using the product. That discomfort stems from questions regarding who owns the data collected and what rights technology providers have to use the data. At the end of the day this is the value proposition I am trying to find: I want to pay a fair and reasonable price for a product that delivers real information for making decisions on my farm in a timely manner and without the fear of my data being used by others without my express permission or in a way that may be ultimately detrimental to my farm or my neighbor's farms.

Ownership Concerns

GiSC is trying to understand this complex world of data and its use. The issue is complicated, and one problem is that one size does not fit all. Deciding on a piece of data collecting equipment, based on its capabilities and features, is challenging enough, much less without the challenge involved in understanding the legalese. The fine print in an end-user license agreement (EULA) regarding my data is very complex. The various EULAs used in the market are so different and diverse that I could not even do justice to the discussion. In some instances, I own the raw data until it is on the provider's servers, but then once the data is stored on those servers, it becomes the provider's data. The provider, in many cases, will promise to never disclose my identity via a process known as anonymization. In many cases these EULAs will include phrases such as: "the grower grants (the service provider) a perpetual worldwide license to the use of any data stored in the system."

GiSC is trying to understand what all this means. Let me be plain when I say that we may need to decide if we, as growers, can accept these EULAs, and the treatment of our data under them, as they are typically structured today. I have tried to hold to an altruist view of what a farmer's rights are in respect to data, but we may need to further investigate if there is potential value by coming to a new conclusion. GiSC and its grower members must decide the data model that brings the most value to the grower's bottom line and is the least disruptive to our world and our trusted partners.

Disruption Concerns

Another challenge facing farmers and the ag tech space are the new players with little understanding of the grower's ecosystem and his network of advisors. An often overused term among technology startups is industry disruption. Technology focused magazines and journals are filled with examples of new companies with game changing platforms that are destined to disrupt entire industries. Disruption is a common theme in tech start-up pitch decks shown to investors as the start-ups seek funding. In the ag tech space, claims such as this or that start-up is going to be the "Amazon of Agriculture". This sounds great to investors, but in truth, most great ideas did not uproot an industry to gain a foot hold. The "old guard" are not the farmer's enemies; they are his support system: the seed dealer, fertilizer dealer, crop insurance agent, banker, equipment salesman, agronomist, entomologist, *et cetera*. This list represents people that the farmer knows on a personal level and contribute to farm's profitability. When problems arise on the farm, farmers can call their agronomist at 10 p.m. or 6 a.m., and he will take their call. Farmers, and the businesses that serve them, are intertwined in a sonnet to produce a crop in a timely manner and at a cost that has them back next year to make new purchases from the vendor. Therefore, we must be cautious when we make blanket, reflexive statements, calling disruption "good". Peter Thiel, PayPal founder and venture capitalist offers this advice in his book "Zero to One":

> "Silicon Valley has become obsessed with 'disruption.' Originally, 'disruption' was a term of art to describe how a firm can use new technology to introduce a low-end product at low prices, improve the product over time, and eventually overtake even the premium products offered by incumbent companies using older technology . . . . However, disruption has recently transmogrified into a self-congratulatory buzzword for anything posing as trendy and new . . . . But if you truly want to make something new, the act of creation is far more impor- tant than the old industries that might not like what you create. Indeed, if your

company can be summed up by its opposition to already existing firms, it can't be completely new . . . ."

Industry Fears

I am borrowing this often-said phrase from others because it is true: "Ag is a small room, but I would not want to paint it." I proceed with caution here, even though a part of me would like to hit "reset" and start over with ag digital technology, including data creation, data collection, data storage, and data analyzation. GiSC has tried to work closely with crop protection companies, input providers, and others with growers as customers, growers who would benefit from utilizing their data and aggregated data, improving those operations through benchmarking and other analytical tools.

I have frankly been confounded by the fact that many, if not most, of these trusted partners of growers are not very open to the idea of their customers integrating the data captured and created via services offered by those trusted partners with other data related to the grower's operation, much less integrating that data in anonymized, aggregated data sets of multiple growers. In fact, many such services require the data captured/created from the service be stored within the service provider's system and only be utilized with the particular service provider's tools. The Ag Tech world is littered with those that live in fear of what a farmer might be able to do with better data. Therefore, most try to create a stand-alone data ecosystem, in which the farmer's data is stored for post-season analysis and creating next year's recommendations. This creates the "data silos" mentioned earlier. That data is never benchmarked against anything, and therefore, the potentially most significant value of such data derived from groups of farmers working together never materializes. In my opinion, if current farm groups don't find a way to move beyond this fear, then Silicon Valley will eventually have a heyday in the ag world, and the disruptions I cautioned against above, will become reality.

Rural Broadband and Connectivity

The last challenge I need to mention involves the continuing need to address the inadequate communications infrastructure in rural areas. While population continues to become more concentrated in the most urban, populated areas, the simple fact remains that those populations' food and fiber continue to be supplied by farms in rural America. The dirt cannot move to town, and we need the means to move the data captured, created, and collected on the farm to "clouds", where the proper analysis can be performed. The rural communications initiatives in the U.S. need to be strengthened if we are going to be part of feeding the world.

I would encourage Congress to continue, and even increase, support of FCC's initiatives including Connect America Fund and Mobility Fund. I understand that serving rural areas requires higher costs, but those costs pale in comparison to the cost of failing to assure adequate communications in rural areas, the price of which is the inability to meet the objective of feeding the world. The current trajectory of total-factor productivity gains in agriculture is inadequate to fill the gap between food production capacity and demand. According to knowledgeable sources, the current gap implies starvation of at least 500M people by 2050, an alarming and totally unacceptable figure. Precision Agriculture advances and other technologies are required to fill that gap, but without new generations of fixed and mobile communications services in the rural areas that produce that food, those productivity gains will not be possible. We must have fast broadband available in rural homes and offices and wireless broadband at the field level with the capability of moving information to and from the cloud for processing, analytics and better decision making.

There is great potential for innovation and entrepreneurship in rural America (Ag and other) but it requires fast Internet connections and 4G wireless services—the same tools that nourish entrepreneurship in metro areas. I make a plea that we cannot afford to deny our potential entrepreneurs and farmers the tools required to assure the maximum contribution to our economy.

Challenges of Digital Ag—Rabobank Summary

I would like to conclude addressing the challenges of digital ag with a profound synopsis of the issue made by Rabobank Senior Research Analyst Kenneth Zuckerberg. In May 2017 Rabobank's RaboResearch issued a report titled "Bungle in the Ag Tech Jungle, Cracking the Code on Precision Farming and Digital Agriculture." The full report is attached as an addendum to this written testimony with the permission of Rabobank Mr. Zuckerberg's summary is as follows:

> "Agriculture has, over the course of its history, embraced new technologies that improve productivity. 'Digital agriculture' represents the latest wave of sector innovation—and while it offers many promising new technologies, farmer

adoption has remained quite modest. The consensus view is that growers will not invest in new/unproven technologies during a cyclical downturn, but there seems to be a bigger limiting factor at work here. This nascent industry has been trying to attract customers before the ecosystem has been properly constructed. What we believe is missing is a standardized way to gather and interpret data, and then translate actionable insights to commercial users—insights which then, in turn, can deliver value to growers. We believe that a standardized system is necessary to drive farmer adoption of digital agriculture services . . . Yet without a common data platform and operating system, it is unlikely that growers, or the vendors providing precision farming services, will fully capture the value associated with digital agriculture."

The Future of Farming: Innovation and Excitement

I can complain every day about all the things that are wrong in the space, but that does not create what I need in my farm operation. The point is that even with problems that seem at times overwhelming, there are nuggets of gold; I find these nuggets all the time as I meet passionate founders of ag tech companies, pioneers who are trying to make a difference. They certainly are capitalist: they want to bring value to the grower and get paid for the value. I am also encouraged by ag groups such as AgGateway and the Open Ag Data Alliance (OADA) who are working to overcome the digital challenges growers face, and am especially encouraged as the ADC and GiSC continue working on behalf of the grower as a vanguard, allowing growers to focus on what they do best—producing a crop.

Innovation is the engine of ever increasing agricultural productivity. As the founder of GiSC, I have the pleasure of seeing innovation happen in exciting new places. On my operation, I have tested many innovative products such as Farmobile's Passive Uplink Connection (PUC), which lets you collect data and seamlessly move it to a cloud regardless of the color of your equipment. For instance, just last week at my farm Blue River Technology tested its "See & Spray" technology, which utilizes computer vision and artificial intelligence to treat weed problems in the field. I see innovation from major technology companies. IBM, as an example, is recruiting and employing highly competent people with expertise in the agriculture industry and has developed powerful weather analytics that can be integrated into digital platforms. Major cellular service providers are also working on applications that leverage their networks to deliver digital tools to growers.

Last, without a doubt, innovation is about to take "front and center" stage around the Internet of Things (IoT), as data collection in ag becomes almost automatic. The handheld computer we all carry around, the smartphone, enabled by IoT sensors on the farm, will provide a leap in the data acquisition landscape. The day of a farmer spending a couple of hours at the end of the day entering data will be a thing of the past; data capture and acquisition will just "happen" as we go about our daily business as farm operators. I am thankful to be seeing the beginning of Ag 3.0, and I would suggest you all stay tuned, because "you ain't seen nothing yet".

Last Words

Somewhere, somehow, in this complex vast world of data utilization, an ecosystem will get built that will overcome the digital ag challenges: the value challenge, the time/resource constraints, and the trepidations of both growers and their trusted partners. Ultimately, this digital ecosystem must be grower-centric and provide for the exchange of information and knowledge, a world where information is not in "data silos" but is available to growers and growers' trusted advisors.

Thank you for the opportunity to speak to you about a topic that I am very passionate. I believe unless we, as farmers, have "stock" in the data we create, in the next decade our world will completely change, or be lost completely. GiSC is a proponent Section 1619 of the 2008 Farm Bill. We are not asking you to make it easier for others to access our USDA information. We appreciate that you understand that there is a right to privacy in our farm locations and our CLUs. Therefore, it would be beneficial to continue to guard the CLU (Common Land Unit) to protect the privacy of America's farmers. Please continue to be supportive of more digital solutions at FSA/RMA, including automating data delivery from USDA to the grower. GiSC is a willing partner in the task, and we will continue to work hand in glove with FSA to try and understand how to keep the grower in control of this digital world. Last, thank you for all the hard work you do for the American Farmer.

ADDENDUM

RaboResearch

Bungle in the Ag Tech Jungle: Cracking the Code on Precision Farming and Digital Agriculture

May 2017

Summary

Agriculture has, over the course of its history, embraced new technologies that improve productivity. 'Digital agriculture' represents the latest wave of sector innovation—and while it offers many promising new technologies, farmer adoption has remained quite modest. The consensus view is that growers will not invest in new/unproven technologies during a cyclical downturn, but there seems to be a bigger limiting factor at work here. This nascent industry has been trying to attract customers before the ecosystem has been properly constructed. What we believe is missing is a standardized way to gather and interpret data, and then translate actionable insights to commercial users—insights which then, in turn, can deliver value to growers. We believe that a standardized system is necessary to drive farmer adoption of digital agriculture services—and within this report, we offer our take on how digital agriculture can add value to production agriculture. Yet without a common data platform and operating system, it is unlikely that growers, or the vendors providing precision farming services, will fully capture the value associated with digital agriculture.

Agricultural Innovation

The Four Waves

The complex process of crop and livestock farming has evolved over the course of thousands of years, and digital agriculture is simply the latest wave of innovation. Advances in farming have historically followed the growth and prosperity of civilization, with mechanization playing an especially prominent role throughout history. The invention of the horse-drawn seed drill in 1700 by Englishman Jethro Tull was notable in that it allowed farmers to plant crops in rows more efficiently than could be done by hand.

Several other useful farm machinery innovations came after the seed drill, namely the cotton gin, reaper/binder, combined harvester-thresher, and gasoline-powered tractor. Collectively, these advances in machine technology fall into a category that we call the first wave of agricultural innovation.

A second wave began in the 1940s, as chemicals used during the war years were repurposed for use in production agriculture. The associated yield benefits of applying nitrogen fertilizer and pesticides incentivized many U.S. farmers to focus on growing few types of crops, but on a much larger scale, abandoning the tradition of farming both crops and livestock. This wave also marked the birth of new farming practices—termed the 'green revolution'—that helped improve crop productivity through more effective usage of synthetic fertilizers and crop production chemicals, as well as field irrigation.

A third innovation wave started in the 1980s and 1990s, a period considered to be the birth of 'precision farming,' a precise sustainability-oriented approach to farming that sought to produce more with fewer inputs and lower environmental impact. The third wave also included gains in plant breeding through genetic engineering and controlled pollination, genetics-based animal breeding, the use of global positioning systems (GPS) on tractors, as well as remote sensing technologies utilizing satellites, drones, and other UAVs.

Digital agriculture is the fourth, and latest, wave of agricultural innovation—and one that has been largely funded by venture capital (VC) investors, along with the VC units of several major F&A and equipment companies. Since the beginning of 2014, over USD $6.5bn of capital has been invested in new precision farming and data-oriented technologies seeking to modernize farming for the digital age. These technologies have taken many shapes, forms, and sizes. These range from cloud-based software tools to hybrid hardware/software products that are 'smart' in that they can communicate with other connected devices wirelessly and digitally, with minimal human intervention.

RaboResearch, Food & Agribusiness, *far.rabobank.com*. Kenneth S. Zuckerberg, Senior Research Analyst, +1 212 916 7998; Dirk Jan Kennes, Global Sector Strategist, +852 21032423.

Table 1: The Four Waves of Agricultural Innovation

Wave	Description
First wave	Mechanization (seed drill, cotton gin, reaper/binder, combined harvester-thresher, tractor)
Second wave	Ag chemistry (nitrogen fertilizer, pesticides)
Third wave	Precision farming (biology, plant and animal genetics, GPS)
Fourth wave	Digital agriculture (smart hardware, analysis of temporal layers of spatial data, weather, and remote sensing to evaluate crop conditions)

Source: Food and Agricultural Organization of the United Nations, USDA, Rabobank 2017.

Another dimension of smart farming involves algorithms, artificial intelligence (AI), and machine learning, which, in essence, combines mathematics, data analytics, and predictive modeling to produce customized recommendations designed to help growers farm more efficiently, sustainably, and profitably.

Figure 1: Investments in Ag Technology (excluding food e-commerce), Q1 2014–Q4 2016

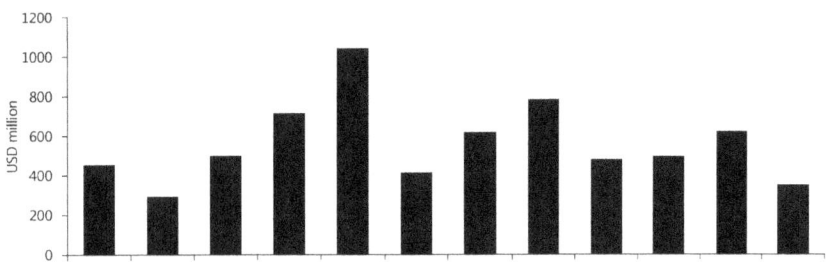

Source: AgFunder AgTech Investing Report (Year in Review 2016) 2017.

These customized recommendations are intended to be precise and prescriptive (building upon the original tenants of precision farming) in that they provide specific advice for managing critical tasks that occur throughout the growing/production season. For crop farmers, the prescriptions conceptually include instructions on what to plant, where and when to plant, what to apply to the soil and the plant (in the form of water, nutrients, and crop protection chemicals), how to most efficiently apply those inputs (*e.g.,* on a variable rate basis), and when to harvest. For dairy and livestock farmers, the prescriptions offer direct guidance on when to feed the animal, provide vitamins and/or medicine, guidance on when to milk and/or when to slaughter, and other herd management matters.

The Promised Value

Digital agriculture offers the promise of greater income and lower volatility, utilizing data, mathematics, and logic to add value to farm decisions by removing human emotion and bias. In crop farming, the 'promised value' for growers consists of optimal financial risk-adjusted returns on the capital used to farm. The idea here being that improved agronomic practices, coupled with more precise field decisions (*e.g.,* the timing and type of nutrient applications) tailored to local field and intra-field conditions, can create the promised value through higher crop yields and lower input costs (for example, lower and more precise nutrient and ag chemical applications), as well as operational efficiencies and time management (automatic, rather than manual collection of helpful data to drive decisions can allow farmers to complete tasks which cannot be automated). Another consideration is better grain quality and consistency, which results in additional value to midstream and downstream buyers.

Below is a partial list of precision and digital technologies currently in use in the global farming community.

Table 2: Leading Precision and Digital Technologies

Auto-steering and guidance systems	Remote sensing (drones, UAVs)
Farm data management software	Satellite imagery (high-resolution)
Crop sensing/measurement	Variable rate technologies
Global positioning systems (GPS)	Yield monitors
Milking robots	Yield maps

Table 2: Leading Precision and Digital Technologies—Continued

| Precision irrigation & water usage monitoring | Wireless weather stations |

Source: Rabobank 2017

Barriers to Adoption

Despite the strong conceptual foundation for using data-intensive tools in agriculture, farmer adoption has been quite low. While there are numerous reasons for this, we highlight five reasons that have been validated in our field research over the past 3 years with growers and data scientists:

- **First, many new software technologies lack a clearly articulated value proposition** and, in fact, are not 'proven' in terms of demonstrating a calculated return or payback on investment. This contrasts with the situation that occurs when new seed technologies come to market, a process in which field trials over multiple growing seasons culminate in a proof of concept, helping to ensure customer trust and subsequent product adoption. Furthermore, we have observed that certain start-up companies and investors have an imperfect understanding of telemetry, artificial intelligence (AI), and data analytics. For example, just because a piece of equipment used in farming is **smart**—it can collect data and transmit data—such data must be further analyzed before it can be translated into an actionable insight.

- **Second, many farms actually lack the necessary technological infrastructure** (enterprise-grade business computing networks, with proper/secure cloud storage and backup), beyond the missing proof of concept, required to interact digitally with industry farm management software systems offered by vendors such as Conservis, Farmers Business Network, Granular, or SST. Trying to get farmers to purchase both IT hardware and software is hard enough in a favorable commodity price environment, as farmers are typically resistant to change, given the 'family tradition' and experience-based nature of farming. Trying to do this during a downturn in the crop cycle (which the industry has been experiencing since commodity prices and farmer income peaked in 2012/13) is, and has been, nearly impossible.

- **Third, selling software as a service (SaaS) to financially strapped farm customers has been a very difficult revenue generation strategy,** given these dynamics. Perhaps a better strategy could be to provide growers basic software without charge, to encourage use and adoption, while selling premium add-on products and services to independent agronomists and crop consultants who advise the growers.

- **Fourth, data ownership and privacy has been a heated, widely debated topic** ever since big data entered the global farming conversation. The matter is actually part of a larger consumer privacy conversation involving medical records, web browsing activities, and the resale of consumer data for use in marketing. An innovative idea to ensure greater privacy is creation of a farmer not-for-profit data cooperative, owned or operated by growers or by an unbiased third party such as an agricultural university. The industry has already seen examples of these ideas in the form of Grower Information Services Cooperative (GiSC) and Ohio State University's Agricultural Data Corporative in the United States. Similar ideas have gained traction in Europe, especially the Netherlands, among both farmer cooperatives, as well as other groups, with a notable example being the Farm-Oriented Open Data in Europe (FOODIE) project in Spain, the Czech Republic, and Germany.

- **Fifth, digital agriculture lacks a universal operating platform** in which to connect the entire ecosystem. At present, digital farming lacks a standardized operating system and/or data platform in which the value chain can upload, store, validate, refine, cleanse, and analyze data and in which relevant stakeholders can easily communicate with each other. Based on our research interviews with data scientists from various enterprise software and business analytics firms—including EMC, IBM, and Verisk—we believe that a data warehouse and data analytics structure (which connects all stakeholders: farmers, software vendors, equipment manufacturers, and data analytics companies, and can enable data sharing) is critical for digital agriculture to add value.

A Framework for Adding Value

Creation of a universal data platform is critical. However, going from the 'concept' stage to the 'blueprint' stage is a complicated exercise. How this happens and who pays for it will depend on which party/parties take leadership in organizing and aligning the industry, and how much capital is set aside for building, testing, and maintaining required systems. Although it took 2 decades for electronic commerce to evolve after Internet access became available to the general public, we would expect creation of the necessary platforms for digital agriculture to occur much faster.

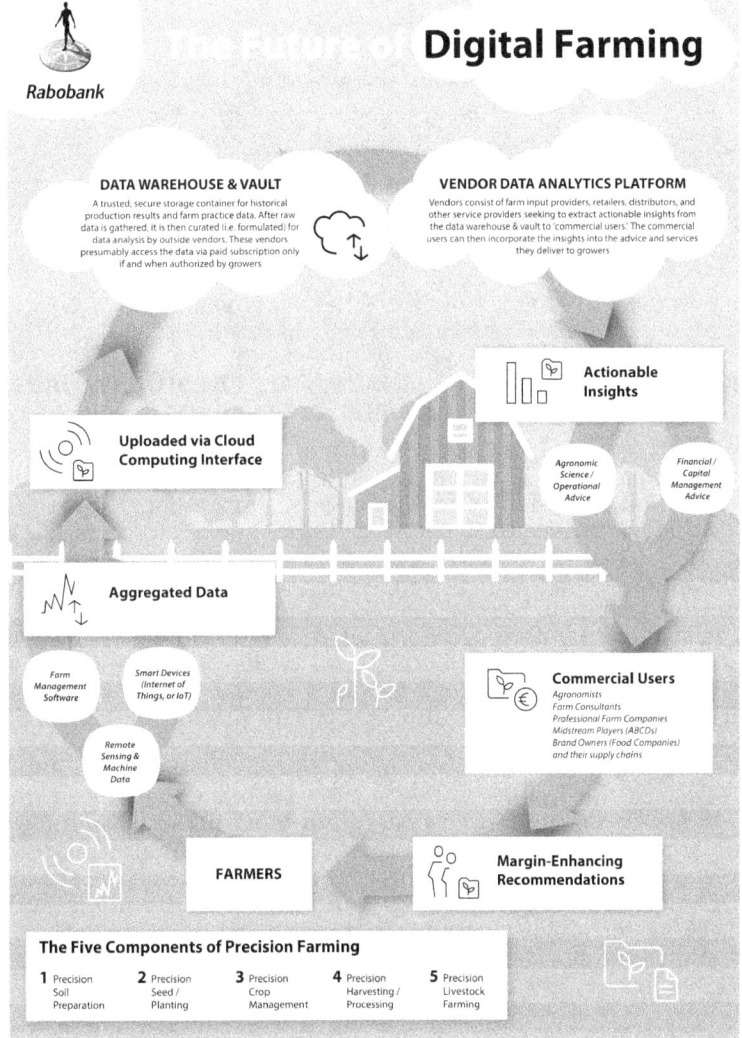

Source: CEMA 2007.

Concluding Thoughts

Digital agriculture represents the newest—and perhaps the most promising—wave of industry innovation that, in our opinion, can help production agriculture operate more efficiently and sustainably, both in terms of long-term financial success and continued environmental stewardship.

While this report approaches the subject of digital agriculture largely from the perspective of upstream farming (crop and livestock) and farm inputs (seeds, crop protection chemicals, fertilizer, and machinery) companies, a common operating system for data gathering, collaboration, and analytics is of critical importance to other players along the value chain.

Midstream food companies and their supply chains (such as processors, storage, and transportation companies) are increasingly demanding more data and information. This is largely driven by the end-consumer who demands greater transparency about the origin of commercially sold food. In our opinion, consumer sentiment and regulations governing the interest of consumers will ultimately guide the further evolution and adoption of digital agriculture.

Imprint

RaboResearch

Food & Agribusiness, *far.rabobank.com.*
Kenneth S. Zuckerberg, Senior Research Analyst, *kenneth.zuckerberg@rabobank.com,* +1 212 916 7998.
Dirk Jan Kennes, Global Sector Strategist, *dirk.jan.kennes@rabobank.com,* +852 21032423.
* 2017—All rights reserved.

This document is meant exclusively for you and does not carry any right of publication or disclosure other than to Coöperative Rabobank U.A. ("Rabobank"), registered in Amsterdam. Neither this document nor any of its contents may be distributed, reproduced, or used for any other purpose without the prior written consent of Rabobank. The information in this document reflects prevailing market conditions and our judgement as of this date, all of which may be subject to change. This document is based on public information. The information and opinions contained in this document have been compiled or derived from sources believed to be reliable, however, Rabobank does not guarantee the correctness or completeness of this document, and does not accept any liability in this respect. The information and opinions contained in this document are indicative and for discussion purposes only. No rights may be derived from any potential offers, transactions, commercial ideas, *et cetera* contained in this document. This document does not constitute an offer, invitation, or recommendation. This document shall not form the basis of, or cannot be relied upon in connection with, any contract or commitment whatsoever. The information in this document is not intended, and may not be understood, as an advice (including, without limitation, an advice within the meaning of article 1:1 and article 4:23 of the Dutch Financial Supervision Act). This document is governed by Dutch law. The competent court in Amsterdam, the Netherlands has exclusive jurisdiction to settle any dispute which may arise out of, or in connection with, this document and/or any discussions or negotiations based on it. This report has been published in line with Rabobank's long-term commitment to international food and agribusiness. It is one of a series of publications undertaken by the global department of RaboResearch Food & Agribusiness.

The CHAIRMAN. Thank you, Mr. Tiller. Very well said.
Mr. Janzen, you are recognized for 5 minutes.

STATEMENT OF TODD J. JANZEN, J.D., PRESIDENT, JANZEN AGRICULTURAL LAW LLC, INDIANAPOLIS, IN

Mr. JANZEN. Good morning, Chairman Crawford, Ranking Member Nolan, and Members of the Subcommittee. My name is Todd Janzen. I am President and attorney of Janzen Agricultural Law LLC, which is a law firm based in Indianapolis, Indiana. And we serve the needs of farmers, agribusiness, and also ag technology providers.

You are going to hear a lot today about agricultural data and this movement of data from on-farm into cloud-based platforms. Yield data is a good example of that. In the past, farmers always kept this data on their farms, and now we are seeing a real movement towards moving that into third-party platform providers that host this data somewhere else.

And together with this movement of data off the farm into the possession of third parties have come a lot of concerns. And groups like American Farm Bureau Federation have taken numerous polls about how farmers feel about this. And in my materials, I have more detail, but I would summarize it by saying there are really three concerns that I see. First, is a lack of trust among farmers in these ag technology providers, because they are giving up part of what makes up their livelihood. Second, is a loss of control to these companies. And third, would be frustrations with the complexity of the legal agreements they are asked to sign.

And, of course, farmers are no strangers to contracts. They sign things all the time. But now they are being asked to check an "I accept" box that has some pretty important consequences for what happens to their data, followed by pages and pages of legal type that they may or may not read.

American Farm Bureau Federation really led an effort a few years ago to come up with some ground rules for how companies should use and control ag data, and this culminated in a document called the Privacy and Security Principles for Farm Data, which I refer to as the Core Principles for farm data. And 37 companies signed onto these and said they were going to implement these core principles in their contracts with farmers. I was fortunate to be involved in those discussions and be part of that as that document came to be.

But just creating Core Principles isn't really enough, because if companies don't follow these Core Principles, we need some way to verify that. And so that is one of the things I want to talk about today.

Farm Bureau, National Farmers Union, and commodity groups for corn, soy, wheat, soybeans, sorghum, and potatoes all came together and formed an organization that could help verify whether or not companies were being transparent with farmers' data. And what they came up with was a way to recognize those companies after going through a certification process. And this is the seal of approval that this organization provides to companies that says Ag Data Transparent. And a company that goes through a certification process can obtain use of that on their marketing materials.

The seal really recognizes companies that have been through a certification process. And in order to get the seal, ten questions are asked of these companies, such as what data are you collecting from farmers, how are you using that data, and then can a farmer retrieve that data back from this company at a later date if they want to.

My role at Janzen Agricultural Law is to administer this project, and that is one reason I am here today. We review these companies' submissions when they fill out these ten question forms, and we check to see are they really being transparent with how they use farmers' ag data.

I am proud to say that eight companies have already been through this certification process and been awarded the Ag Data Transparent seal. In fact, MyAgData, Deb Casurella's company, was the very first one to obtain use of the seal. But there are still many more that could go through and become certified, and we hope that they do.

We also post the answers to these ten questions when companies go through the process online at *agdatatransparent.com,* and in my materials I have a lot more detail about that.

I will just conclude by saying there is still a lot of work to be done here. There are still a lot of companies that should go through the certification process but haven't as of today. There are still a lot of complex, complicated contracts that farmers are asked to sign, and we can do better as a legal community to address that as well.

I hope that when different companies come before you as a Committee you will ask them, do you have the Ag Data Transparent seal? Or if companies have been through the process, you will congratulate them for achieving that.

I am honored to speak with you here today about this effort and the work that I do, and I welcome your questions later today. Thank you.

[The prepared statement of Mr. Janzen follows:]

PREPARED STATEMENT OF TODD J. JANZEN, J.D., PRESIDENT, JANZEN AGRICULTURAL LAW LLC, INDIANAPOLIS, IN

Good morning, Chairman Crawford, Ranking Member Nolan, and Members of Subcommittee. My name is Todd J. Janzen, I am the President and attorney with

Janzen Agricultural Law, LLC, a law firm based in Indianapolis, Indiana that serves the needs of America's farmers, ag technology providers, and agribusinesses.

One of the reasons we founded Janzen Ag Law in 2015 was that we wanted to be at the forefront of the changes that have been occurring on the farm for the past few years. Farms are becoming more digital every day, and together with that digitalization is a movement of agricultural data stored on computers in the farm office to cloud-based data storage devices. Agricultural data (ag data) can be many things, including yield data, soil data, planting information, weather data, financial data, *etc.* This marks the first time in history that the majority of the information that farmers generate and use on their farms has been moved into the hands of companies outside the farm.

As a result, we are seeing a digital land-rush occurring across the United States. The past few years have seen millions of dollars pour into ag data startups from Silicon Valley to Kansas City. Historic legacy agricultural companies, such as John Deere, are also at the forefront of this movement by expanding their product offerings to include cloud-based data storage platforms. All of these companies are scrambling to get the most acres of data into their platforms so that when consolidation of ag technology providers (ATPs) begins, they are in the strongest position.

In the race to the cloud, we must also be cautious so that the American farmer is not left behind. Today I will address the issues facing farmers as digitalization occurs and how the industry has begun to address these issues.

Issues Facing Farmers as Ag Data Moves into the Cloud

American Farm Bureau Federation (Farm Bureau) conducted a poll of over 400 farmers in 2016 to understand their issues concerning ag data privacy, security, and control. The poll highlighted what are essentially three issues that continue to come up when asking farmers about ag data concerns:

1. Lack of Trust

Seventy-seven percent (77%) of farmers expressed concern about which entities can access their farm data after the data is uploaded to cloud-based servers. The same percentage expressed concern about whether uploading the data could cause it to be used for regulatory purposes.

Sixty-seven percent (67%) of farmers said they consider how outside parties will use their ag data when deciding whether to entrust their data with a certain ATP.

A farmer's lack of trust can come from many sources, but I speculate it originates in two places. Many ag data companies are new. Ag data startups lack the goodwill that older agricultural companies have spent years building. They have new sales associates who are strangers to the farm, or in some instances, strangers to agriculture. They are viewed as outsiders.

Older, long-established agricultural companies do not suffer from a general lack of trust with the farmer, since they have spent years building that relationship. But when a seed company, equipment manufacturer, or ag retailer begins offering an ag data platform to store the farmer's ag data, farmers often are skeptical about whether the storage provider is trying to help the farmer raise a better crop or using the ag data to sell the farmer more or higher-priced goods and services. This skepticism may erode a farmer's trust.

2. Concern with Losing Control

Farmers are also concerned that uploading their ag data to cloud-based platforms means they will lose control over downstream uses. Sixty-six percent (66%) of respondents in the Farm Bureau poll believe farmers should share in the potential financial benefits from the use of their data beyond the direct value they may realize on their farm.

Farmers raised concerns that ATPs could use their ag data to gain an unfair advantage in the marketplace. Sixty-one percent (61%) of farmers expressed worry that ATPs could use their data to influence market decisions.

These concerns arise from a fundamental legal truth about ag data—there are no laws that specifically protect farmers' privacy and security concerns. Ag data is not typically "personally identifiable information," such that it would be protected by state laws which prevent misuse of personal information like name, address, and phone number. Nor does ag data fit into a class of data that Congress has chosen to protect legally, such as medical information (HIPAA). Finally, ag data does not neatly fit into existing legal protections for intellectual property, such as patents, trademarks, or copyrights. Ag data ultimately may be deemed a trade secret under existing state and Federal trade secret laws, but that will depend upon whether courts interpret existing statutes to include information such as agronomic data.

These uncertainties mean that the contracts between farmers and ag tech providers are very important. These contracts will determine farmers' rights in the ag data their farms create.

3. Frustration with Complexity of Current Legal Agreements

Fifty-nine (59%) percent of farmers were confused about whether current legal agreements allowed ATPs to use their ag data to market other services, equipment, or inputs back to them. Zippy Duvall, President of Farm Bureau, said: "This indicates a higher level of clarity and transparency is needed to secure grower confidence. One of the topics I hear most about from farmers on the data issue is having a clear understanding about the details of 'Terms and Conditions' and 'Privacy Policy' documents we all sign when buying new electronics. You should not have to hire an attorney before you are comfortable signing a contract with an ag technology provider."

Our experience as a law firm working in this area confirms that this is a real problem for farmers and ATPs. There is no standard agreement that governs ag data transfer, use, and control by ATPs. Instead, technology companies have adapted other forms of legal agreements to try to address the issues associated with moving ag data into cloud-based platforms, but with limited success. A farmer seeking to compare two similar products today might find that they are governed by two very different sets of contracts.

This only adds to a farmer's confusion. If we want to make technology easy to embrace and use—and we do—then we need to simplify the contracts farmers sign when implementing new ag data technology on the farm.

How the Industry Is Addressing Farmers' Concerns

1. The Privacy and Security Principles for Farm Data

Farm Bureau, National Farmer's Union, and national commodity organizations for corn, soybeans, wheat, and sorghum, led an effort in 2014 to establish fundamental principles for companies working in the ag data space. These organizations held a series of meetings where roundtable discussions occurred among industry stakeholders, such as John Deere, CNH Industrial, AGCO, Monsanto, DuPont Pioneer, Beck's Hybrids, Dow Agrosciences, Farmobile, and other ag technology providers. The culmination of these efforts was the drafting of the "Privacy and Security Principles for Farm Data," also known as ag data's "Core Principles."

The Core Principles address thirteen key elements related to ag data. These include:

- Education.
- Ownership.
- Collection, Access and Control.
- Notice.
- Transparency and Consistency.
- Choice.
- Portability.
- Terms and Definitions.
- Disclosure, Use, and Sale Limitation.
- Data Retention and Availability.
- Contract Termination.
- Unlawful or Anti-Competitive Activities.
- Liability & Security Safeguards.

After releasing the Core Principles in 2014, Farm Bureau asked companies to voluntarily "sign on" to the document. As of July 2017, the following organizations and companies have agreed to implement the Core Principles into their contracts with farmers.

AGCO
Ag Connections, Inc.
Agrible, Inc.*
AgSense
AgWorks
Ag Leader Technology
American Farm Bureau Fed.
American Soybean Assoc.
Beck's Hybrids *
CNH Industrial
Conservis *
Crop IMS
DuPont Pioneer
Farm Dog
Farmobile LLC *
Granular *
Grower Information Services Cooperative
GROWMARK, Inc.*
Independent Data Management LLC *
John Deere
Mapshots, Inc.
National Assoc. of Wheat Growers
National Barley Growers Assoc.
National Corn Growers Assoc.
National Farmers Union
National Potato Council
National Sorghum Producers
North American Equipment Dealers Assoc.
OnFarm
Raven Industries
Reinke Manufacturing Co., Inc.
Syngenta
The Climate Corporation—a division of Monsanto
USA Rice Federation
Valley Irrigation

CropMetrics   National Cotton Council   ZedX Inc.
Dow AgroSciences LLC

* Company certified to be Ag Data Transparent. For more information, visit *www.agdatatransparent.com*.

A copy of the Core Principles is attached as *Exhibit A*.

2. The Ag Data Transparent Effort

Having the Core Principles in place was a great starting point for the ag data industry to address farmers' concerns with ag data privacy, use, and control. However, the Core Principles are only guidelines, and only valuable if companies incorporate the Core Principles into their contracts with farmers. Therefore, following the release of the Core Principles, several farm groups and industry stakeholders worked together to create an independent verification tool that could help farmers determine if ag tech providers are abiding by the Core Principles. This tool is called the Ag Data Transparency Evaluator. It is a simple three-step process:

- Participating companies must answer ten questions about how they store, use, and transfer ag data.
- The ten question answer form is reviewed by an independent third party for transparency and completeness.
- If the evaluation is acceptable, the company is awarded the "Ag Data Transparent" seal of approval for use on its future marketing materials.

Participation is voluntary, but all companies that signed onto the Core Principles have been asked to participate in the Ag Data Transparent effort as well.

a. *The 10 Question Evaluation*

Here is a list of the ten questions that each participant is asked to answer as part of the evaluation:

1. What categories of data does the product or service collect from me (the farmer)?
2. Do the Ag Technology Provider's (ATP's) agreements address ownership of my data after my data is transferred to the ATP?
3. If the ATP contracts with other companies to provide data related services, does the ATP require these companies to adhere to the ATP's privacy policies with me?
4. Will the ATP obtain my consent before providing other companies with access to my data?
5. After I upload data to the ATP, will it be possible to retrieve my original complete dataset in an original or equivalent format?
6. Will the ATP notify me when its agreements change?
7. Will the ATP notify me if a breach of data security occurs that causes disclosure of my data to an outside party?
8. Upon my request, can my original dataset be deleted when my contract with the ATP terminates?
9. Do the ATP's agreements establish how long my original datasets will be retained?
10. Do the ATP's agreements address what happens to my data if the ATP is sold to another company?

Answers to all questions except for question 1 are "yes" or "no," but companies are also given space to explain their answer.

b. *Reviewing the 10 Question Evaluation*

After an ag tech company completes the ten question evaluation form, the company submits its answers to an independent third party evaluator to determine compliance. Janzen Agricultural Law LLC is the law firm that has been selected to conduct the evaluations. After reviewing a company's answers, we typically go back to that company with suggestions for improving its contracts and policies to bring into compliance with Core Principles. Companies then make those revisions to their contracts and policies and resubmit their ten question form. Once a company's answers align with the Core Principles, we send an official letter designating the company as "Ag Data Transparent" and authorizing use of the seal of approval.

The final, approved ten question answer forms are posted on the Ag Data Transparent website at *www.AgDataTransparent.com* Farmers can research and review companies' answers online. The website requires no log in and is free to use. An example of the home page is attached as *Exhibit B*.

c. ***The Ag Data Transparent Seal of Approval***

Companies that undergo evaluation and are approved as "Ag Data Transparent" may then use the seal of approval on their websites and marketing materials. To date, eight companies have completed the evaluation and been approved as "Ag Data Transparent." These eight companies are:

- AgIntegrated, Inc.
- Agrible, Inc.
- Beck's Hybrids.
- Conservis Corporation.
- Farmobile.
- Granular.
- GROWMARK.
- Independent Data Management LLC.

The participants are diverse, from a Silicon Valley ag tech startup, to a Midwestern seedcompany, to one of the nation's largest farm cooperatives and ag retailers. These companiesmay use the Ag Data Transparent seal on their websites, denoting their compliance with theCore Principles. Farmers who see the seal of approval will know the company went through thetime and effort to certify its contract.

The Ag Data Transparent process addresses farmers' three main concerns with ag data. First, the process instills trust. No company submits its contracts to a voluntary evaluation unless the company is willing to revise its contracts, as necessary, to bring them into compliance with the Core Principles. Second, loss of control is addressed by requiring tech providers to obtain farmer consent before transferring data to third parties. Finally, farmers' complexity frustration is addressed by condensing all of a tech provider's contracts into a ten question form that answers the questions farmers want to know. The Ag Data Transparent process makes contracts better.

d. ***Who is behind the Ag Data Transparent effort?***

The Ag Data Transparent effort is governed by a nonprofit corporation, the Ag Data Transparency Evaluator Inc. The corporate bylaws create two classes of directors: (1) farm organizations that are made up of farmer-member organizations; and (2) diverse ag technology providers, referred to as "industry partners." The farm organizations are American Farm Bureau Federation, American Soybean Association, National Corn Growers Association, National Farmers Union, National Sorghum Producers, National Association of Wheat Growers and National Potato Council. The industry partner board members are ag technology providers ranging from large corporations, medium-sized companies, and ag tech startup organizations.

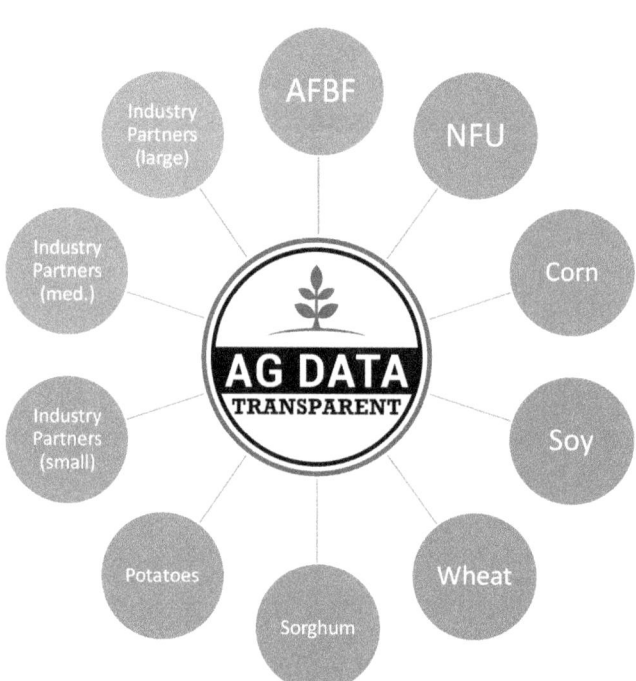

Janzen Agricultural Law LLC, which serves as the administrator of the program and conducts the evaluation reviews, is not a board member.

3. The Ag Data Use Policy

Our law firm also drafts terms of service, license agreements, privacy polices, and other contracts for ag technology providers. This work has confirmed many concerns facing farmers today when it comes to ag data. We see how companies struggle to communicate clearly how they intend to store, use, and transfer ag data.

For these reasons, we have encouraged companies to draft "data use policies" or "data use agreements" for their farmers. In a data use contract, the technology provider addresses all of the issues raised by the ten questions and the Core Principles. For example, a data use policy will explain what information the provider collects and what permission is required before the provider transfers that data to another party.

From our standpoint, the Ag Data Transparent effort has helped drive more technology providers into creating data use policies. Thus, the effort has paid dividends even for some companies that have not participated in evaluations because it has caused them to rethink how they are contracting with farmers.

Conclusion

The Ag Data Transparent effort is great step towards bringing transparency to ag data contracts between farmers and their technology providers. Wider participation would certainly help the effort, but that is up to the industry. Out of the dozens of ag tech providers with cloud-based platforms on the market today, only eight have embraced the process. To be fair, others are in the process but adoption could still be faster and better.

Farmers should ask their technology providers why they have not earned that Ag Data Transparent seal. This Subcommittee should ask technology providers this question as well when they come before you to testify.

Thank you, Mr. Chairman, for your time and attention to this important issue. I look forward to answering any questions you may have for me.

TODD J. JANZEN, Janzen Agricultural Law LLC.

Exhibit A

Privacy and Security Principles for Farm Data

(Ag Data's Core Principles)

November 2014

The recent evolution of precision agriculture and farm data is providing farmers with tools, which can help to increase productivity and profitability.

As that technology continues to evolve, the undersigned organizations and companies believe the following data principles should be adopted by each Agriculture Technology Provider (ATP).

It is imperative that an ATP's principles, policies and practices be consistent with each company's contracts with farmers. The undersigned organizations are committed to ongoing engagement and dialogue regarding this rapidly developing technology.

Education: Grower education is valuable to ensure clarity between all parties and stakeholders. Grower organizations and industry should work to develop programs, which help to create educated customers who understand their rights and responsibilities. ATPs should strive to draft contracts using simple, easy to understand language.

Ownership: We believe farmers own information generated on their farming operations. However, it is the responsibility of the farmer to agree upon data use and sharing with the other stakeholders with an economic interest, such as the tenant, landowner, cooperative, owner of the precision agriculture system hardware, and/or ATP, *etc.* The farmer contracting with the ATP is responsible for ensuring that only the data they own or have permission to use is included in the account with the ATP.

Collection, Access and Control: An ATP's collection, access and use of farm data should be granted only with the affirmative and explicit consent of the farmer. This will be by contract agreements, whether signed or digital.

Notice: Farmers must be notified that their data is being collected and about how the farm data will be disclosed and used. This notice must be provided in an easily located and readily accessible format.

Transparency and Consistency: ATPs shall notify farmers about the purposes for which they collect and use farm data. They should provide information about how farmers can contact the ATP with any inquiries or complaints, the types of third parties to which they disclose the data and the choices the ATP offers for limiting its use and disclosure.

An ATP's principles, policies and practices should be transparent and fully consistent with the terms and conditions in their legal contracts. An ATP will not change the customer's contract without his or her agreement.

Choice: ATPs should explain the effects and abilities of a farmer's decision to opt in, opt out or disable the availability of services and features offered by the ATP. If multiple options are offered, farmers should be able to choose some, all, or none of the options offered. ATPs should provide farmers with a clear understanding of what services and features may or may not be enabled when they make certain choices.

Portability: Within the context of the agreement and retention policy, farmers should be able to retrieve their data for storage or use in other systems, with the exception of the data that has been made anonymous or aggregated and is no longer specifically identifiable. Non-anonymized or non-aggregated data should be easy for farmers to receive their data back at their discretion.

Terms and Definitions: Farmers should know with whom they are contracting if the ATP contract involves sharing with third parties, partners, business partners, ATP partners, or affiliates. ATPs should clearly explain the following definitions in a consistent manner in all of their respective agreements: (1) farm data; (2) third party; (3) partner; (4) business partner; (5) ATP partners; (6) affiliate; (7) data account holder; (8) original customer data. If these definitions are not used, ATPs should define each alternative term in the contract and privacy policy. ATPs should strive to use clear language for their terms, conditions and agreements.

Disclosure, Use and Sale Limitation: An ATP will not sell and/or disclose non-aggregated farm data to a third party without first securing a legally binding commitment to be bound by the same terms and conditions as the ATP has with the farmer. Farmers must be notified if such a sale is going to take place and have the option to opt out or have their data removed prior to that sale. An ATP will not share or disclose original farm data with a third party in any manner that is inconsistent with the contract with the farmer. If the agreement with the third party is not the same as the agreement with the ATP, farmers must be presented with the third party's terms for agreement or rejection.

Data Retention and Availability: Each ATP should provide for the removal, secure destruction and return of original farm data from the farmer's account upon the request of the farmer or after a pre-agreed period of time. The ATP should include a requirement that farmers have access to the data that an ATP holds during that data retention period. ATPs should document personally identifiable data retention and availability policies and disposal procedures, and specify requirements of data under policies and procedures.

Contract Termination: Farmers should be allowed to discontinue a service or halt the collection of data at any time subject to appropriate ongoing obligations. Procedures for termination of services should be clearly defined in the contract.

Unlawful or Anti-Competitive Activities: ATPs should not use the data for unlawful or anticompetitive activities, such as a prohibition on the use of farm data by the ATP to speculate in commodity markets.

Liability & Security Safeguards: The ATP should clearly define terms of liability. Farm data should be protected with reasonable security safeguards against risks such as loss or unauthorized access, destruction, use, modification or disclosure. Polices for notification and response in the event of a breach should be established. The undersigned organizations for the Privacy and Security Principles of Farm Data as of April 1, 2016.

AGCO	DuPont Pioneer	National Potato Council
Ag Connections, Inc.	Farm Dog	National Sorghum Producers
Agrible, Inc.*	Farmobile LLC *	North American Equipment Dealers Association
AgSense	Granular *	
AgWorks	Grower Information Services Cooperative	OnFarm
Ag Leader Technology	GROWMARK, Inc.*	Raven Industries
American Farm Bureau Federation	Independent Data Management LLC *	Reinke Manufacturing Co., INC.
American Soybean Association	John Deere	Syngenta
Beck's Hybrids *	Mapshots, Inc.	The Climate Corporation—a division of Monsanto
CNH Industrial	National Association of Wheat Growers	
Conservis *	National Barley Growers Association	USA Rice Federation
Crop IMS	National Corn Growers Association	Valley Irrigation
CropMetrics	National Cotton Council	ZedX Inc.
Dow AgroSciences LLC	National Farmers Union	

* Company that has also certified its policy is compliant with the Ag Data Transparency Evaluator. For more information, visit *www.agdatatransparent.com*.

Exhibit B

Ag Data Transparent Homepage (*www.AgDataTransparent.com*)

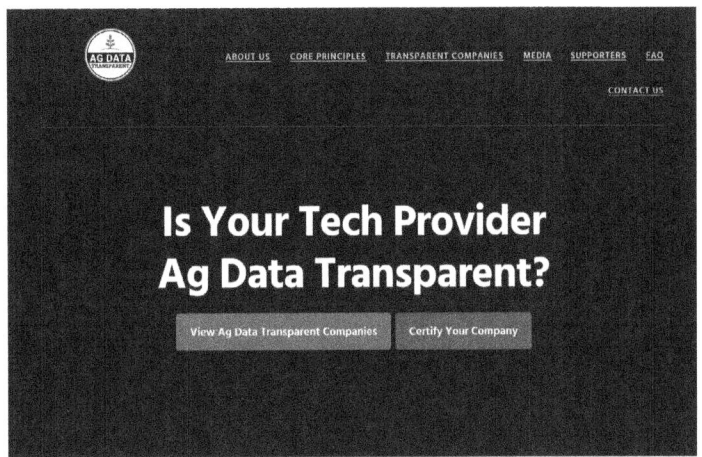

The Core Principles Behind the Ag Data Transparent Seal

Many farm organizations have identified ag data privacy, security, and control are important issues for their farmers. With the help of ag technology providers, these farm groups have created the Ag Data Core Principles to address these issues. The Ag Data Transparent Seal recognizes companies who follow the Ag Data Core Principles and submit their contracts and policies to an independent evaluation to determine compliance.

10 Questions Determine Compliance with Our Core Principles

The Ag Data Transparent Seal represents transparency, simplicity, and trust. Ag technology companies that have been awarded the Seal have answered 10 basic questions about how they use farmers' ag data. The answers are verified by a third party. When a farmer sees the Seal on a product, that farmer knows that ag tech provider voluntarily submitted their company's contracts and policies for evaluation.

How Companies Can Obtain the Ag Data Transparent Seal

Any ag technology company can obtain the Seal by undertaking a certification process. After agreeing to participate, the company must answer the 10 questions about how it uses farmers' ag data. Next, the company must submit its answers, contracts, and policies to an administrator for an independent, third-party review. Companies that pass the review are awarded the Seal for one year and their answers are posted on this website.

The CHAIRMAN. Thank you, Mr. Janzen.

Ms. Casurella, you are recognized for 5 minutes.

STATEMENT OF DEBORAH CASURELLA, CHIEF EXECUTIVE OFFICER, INDEPENDENT DATA MANAGEMENT, LLC, HUDSON, WI

Ms. CASURELLA. Thanks for the opportunity to be here today. I am going to talk about production agriculture, also known as precision ag, its impact on farmers, the USDA, and crop insurance companies.

A key way to help farmers, the government, and taxpayers realize the benefits of precision ag technology is to open the third-party channel and allow producers to report from home. This can be done with commercial software, much like the IRS did in 1986, by allowing taxpayers to use products like TurboTax to report their acres. To me, the most impressive pieces of precision ag are the sensors connected to control systems that run the equipment. This technology allows farmers to achieve better yields, use fewer resources, and reduce the impact on the environment, and ultimately meet world food demand.

The adoption rate is increasing. Estimates say that precision ag is already used on 70 percent of acres. A significant byproduct is data.

Farmers and ranchers are collecting all sorts of information, but they are last to the trough to get benefits from their own data. Both FSA and crop insurance agents require farmers to submit an annual report of farm acres, but we don't make it easy for them. Farmers who use precision ag start with an electronic version of their planting information, including the exact geographic location of each and every seed in the ground. The current reporting process will see that data translated somewhere between three and eight times back and forth between tabular data and maps, from electronic to paper and back, all to end up in electronic form where it started, but in government systems.

For 7 years, the USDA has been working on a new system to share common information electronically between agencies. For the past 3 crop years, farmers have been able to report the common information just once, either to the FSA or their crop insurance agent, and have that information electronically shared with the other. This is a good step and a direct result of the Acreage Crop Reporting Streamlining Initiative, ACRSI, which was reauthorized in the 2014 Farm Bill.

The reporting standards for RMA and FSA include geospatial data, the map, along with crop and acreage information, but much of that information is not required, which causes two problems. First, even if a crop insurance agent collects the geospatial data, and many do, they don't provide it to the FSA because it is not required. And second, FSA and RMA don't exchange that optional data, the maps, with each other. Because the data is incomplete, the other agency doesn't use it.

Frustrated farmers must still visit both the FSA county office and their crop insurance agent and share the same information to complete reporting. Three main reasons for the visit. First, farmers must validate and sign their acreage report in each office. Second, farmers must provide program-specific information to the second agency that wasn't collected by the first agency. And third, farmers need to complete their maps.

The USDA knows it is a problem and is actively working on it. In 2015, as part of the ACRSI initiative, FSA conducted a pilot for electronic acreage reporting using precision ag data. One of the things the pilot tested was allowing farmers to use third-party commercial software to report their acres. Independent Data Management, using MyAgData, was selected to test that channel, and the pilot was an overwhelming success. MyAgData was a bridge, because it included words, numbers, and maps, not just the required data but also the optional data, and one report could be used for both FSA and RMA.

Because the data was more precise, participants reported an average of 4.7 percent fewer acres. That means a lower insurance premium for the farmer, decreased premium subsidy funded by taxpayers, lower indemnity for crop insurance companies and the RMA, and a reduction in claims because yield was not diluted across unplanted acres.

Think of the numbers with expanded use. If 25 percent of the acres were reported using a grower's actual field boundaries, and the average reported acres were 4.7 lower, producer premiums and taxpayer subsidies could be reduced by up to $179 million annually. That is a conservative number, but $179 million is a reasonable number to expect with 25 percent of acres.

And that is only insurance premiums. What are the savings on indemnities? What if this also applied to farm programs?

Again, just using map tools to do reporting changed the agency's visit length from hours to minutes, and despite the success the third-party channel remains closed.

USDA can accept the standard. They share it between agencies today. Both FSA and RMA understand the benefits, and the FSA union supports it. All that is required are minor system changes.

Farmers plant fields. Let them report what they plant. It is more accurate. It saves time and money for farmers and the agencies and it saves taxpayer dollars.

Complete accurate data is the lifeblood of farm programs, crop insurance, and conservation programs. The data is already being collected. Let's use it.

Thank you.

[The prepared statement of Ms. Casurella follows:]

PREPARED STATEMENT OF DEBORAH CASURELLA, CHIEF EXECUTIVE OFFICER, INDEPENDENT DATA MANAGEMENT, LLC, HUDSON, WI

The company was founded in 2012 and funded primarily by farmers to provide technology to make it easier for farmers to submit acreage reports to the USDA. That sounds pretty simple, but like many things in agriculture, it is a bit more complicated than it appears.

We started with software that could take data from a wide variety of precision ag equipment (about 110 different formats), translate that data into usable annotated maps, overlay the government's description of the field called a Common Land Unit (CLU) on the map, give the farmer tools to review and fill in any missing data and print documents that the farmer could take to their crop insurance agent or the Farm Services Agency (FSA) and report. We've grown into a full function acreage reporting suite of tools including a mobile version that allows data capture in the field.

I have over 30 years of hands on experience delivering practical operations and information technology solutions to solve real business problems. I have worked in environments ranging from small startups to large multinationals in insurance (including crop insurance), transportation and health care.

I chaired the AgGateway data privacy policy committee that, together with American Farm Bureau Federation produced the first widely recognized set of privacy standards for ag data. AgGateway is a leading ag industry group. Those privacy standards have been largely adopted by more than 50 ag technology companies.

I am going to talk about precision agriculture (precision ag) technology, how that technology has impacted farmers and their interactions with government programs, USDA and the crop insurance companies and I will suggest that a key way to help farmers, the government and the taxpayers realize some of the potential benefits that have been unlocked is to open the third party channel for acreage reporting and give farmers the option to report from home using commercial off-the-shelf (COTS) software much like the IRS did in 1986 by allowing taxpayers to use products like Turbo Tax and other third party software to report income tax.

In 2009, I became CIO of an Approved Insurance Provider (AIP) and was surprised at the widespread use of technology in farming. Most impressive are the control systems that run the equipment and the precision agriculture instrumentation that guides them to allow farmers to achieve better yields, use fewer resources, and reduce the impact on the environment.

The adoption rate of this technology is increasing. Some estimates say precision ag is already used on close to 70% of crop acres.

One of the significant by-products is data. Farmers and ranchers are collecting all sorts of information about their operation, but they are last to the trough to get benefits from their own data. The "big ag" companies and equipment manufacturers find ways to collect and aggregate data and use it to their advantage but the application of farm data to directly benefit the average farmer is rare.

When I refer to tabular data, I mean words and numbers. When I talk about geospatial data, think maps.

The Farm Service Agency (FSA) requires farmers and ranchers participating in their programs to submit an annual report on all cropland use on their farms. Crop insurance agents for providers approved by the USDA Risk Management Agency (RMA) also require these reports. But we don't make it easy for the farmer. For years, farmers and ranchers have been required to enter the common information from their acreage reports at both the county FSA office and at their crop insurance agent's office.

Farmers using precision ag start with an electronic version of their planting information including the exact geographic location of each and every seed in the ground. The current reporting process will see that precise data translated somewhere between three and eight times, back and forth between tabular data and maps and from electronic formats to paper and back, all to end up in electronic form (where it started) in the government systems.

For the past 7 years, USDA has been working on a new system to better collaborate and streamline the collection of common information that can be securely and electronically shared between FSA and the Risk Management Agency (RMA). For the past 3 crop years, farmers and ranchers been able to provide the common information from their acreage reports just once—either to FSA or to their crop insurance agent—and have that common information securely and electronically shared with the other. This is a direct result of USDA's Acreage Crop Reporting Streamlining Initiative (ACRSI) which was reauthorized in the 2014 Farm Bill.

The reporting standard for both RMA and FSA includes geospatial data (maps) along with regular crop and acreage information but much of it is not required. This causes at least two problems. First, even if a crop insurance company collects the geospatial data (and some do), they don't provide it as part of their report because it is not required. And second, FSA and RMA do not require the exchange of optional data with each other. This means that the interagency exchanged data is usually ignored because, to use the data, each agency requires some of the optional data. The end result is that frustrated farmers must visit both the FSA county office and their crop insurance agent's office and share the same information to complete reporting.

There are three main reasons for this:

1. Farmers must validate and sign their respective acreage reports in each office. Electronic signature is accepted in crop insurance, but not yet in FSA reporting.
2. Farmers must provide the program-specific information to the second agency that was not required to report to the first agency.
3. Farmers must complete maps (the geospatial data).

USDA knows this is a problem and has been actively working on it. In 2015, as part of USDA's Acreage Crop Reporting Streamlining Initiative (ACRSI), the FSA conducted a pilot for electronic acreage reporting. One of the things the pilot tested was allowing farmers to use third party commercial software to report their acres. Independent Data Management, using MyAgData→ participated as the 3rd party software provider and the pilot was an overwhelming success on several levels:

Farmers that reported using precision ag data saw an average of 4.7% fewer acres reported. The increased accuracy of precision ag data meant a lower crop insurance premium for the farmer, decreased premium subsidies funded by taxpayers, lower indemnity for crop insurance companies and the Risk Management Agency (RMA), and a reduction in claims as yield was not diluted across unplanted acres. Ultimately this will result in higher guarantees for a producer. Think of the numbers with expanded use. If 25% of acres were reported using a grower's accurate field boundaries and the average was a reduction of reported acres of 4.74%, producer annual premiums and taxpayer subsidies could be reduced by up to $179M. That's only crop insurance premium. What are the savings on indemnities? What if this also applied to farm programs?

The third party software provided the bridge because its reporting included not just the required data, but also the optional data and one reporting could be used for both FSA and RMA.

Just using map-based tools to do either precision ag based reporting or electronic manual reporting provided a big reduction in the effort involved to report for the farmers and for USDA.

Despite this success, the third party channel remains closed.

USDA can accept electronic transmissions from any third party. The standards have been out to the ag industry for a year and used for 3 years by the agencies. The FSA and Risk Management Agency (RMA) both understand the benefits. The National Association of FSA County Office Employees (NASCOE) has been supportive of ACRSI. All that is required are minor system changes and a policy change to open the third party channel for reporting.

Farmers plant fields. Let them report what they plant. It is more accurate, saves them time and money, saves the agencies time and money and saves taxpayer money. And the more accurate data helps not only current programs, but future ones be more effective and more efficient saving even more time and money.

Thank you.

Fields as Planted by a Producer

Taxpayer paid subsidies and benefits for crop insurance and farm programs could bereduced by 4.73% if acres were collected using a producers['] electronic field boundaries.

Producer Fields & Common Land Units (CLUs)

White lines are the producer's CLUs.
Yellow represents planted corn, dark green is beans, red hashing is crop planted outside of a CLU, light green is idle ground with a CLU.

One Producers Story (Anonymous Blog Post) Page 1

Customer Connection: Certifying- Can it REALLY be *THAT Painful?*   6 July 2015

Complaining? Who's complaining?

I often hear people joking that as farmers, we like to complain about everything. It hasn't rained – so we complain. It has rained too much – so we complain. Crop prices are high but our yields are low – so we complain. Our yields are high but crop prices are low- so we complain. Equipment, fertilizer, seed costs... way too much, so we complain. And *SOMETIMES*, I admit we might be blowing hot air. However, one complaint is definitely legit – and I can say that because I experienced it firsthand, in the flesh last week. Which one? Certifying acres. I went in thinking "how bad can it be???" I came out shaking my head and mentally exhausted.

Here is the skinny on acre certification. Each year, farmers are required to go into their local county FSA (Farm Service Agency, which is a division of the US Department of Agriculture or USDA) office to verify our crops and acres. We do this post-plant so we can accurately report the number of acres, type of crop and planting date for each field. If we don't certify, we won't be eligible for any applicable federal crop insurance or generalized Farm Programs. It really shouldn't be too difficult given that most farmers keep accurate records of each field (whether documented via GPS or manually). We simply have to verify and sign. Easy peasy (as my kids would say). Or Not.

I would like to begin by saying this blog is in no way a reflection on the kind ladies in the FSA office who helped us. They were terrific - and nearly as frustrated as we were. Our original appointment was for 3:00pm in Oakland, IA- about 35 minutes away. See, you certify at the FSA office in the county that your farms are in... so for the portion of our operation that is in Pottawattamie County, we go to Oakland and then to Atlantic for our Cass county farms. Anyway, ▮▮▮▮ my husband) was delivering corn to the elevator and wound up 10 trucks deep in line to unload. As a result, we pushed our time slot back and it was nearly 4:00 before we arrived. Unfortunately, they close at 4:30.

We brought along our planting data from our GS3 GreenStar™ monitors, which show the date and acre quantity of all of the fields we planted. Keep in mind that "field" is as we (the farmer) define it. Upon arrival, they handed us several satellite imagery pictures of our farms. First step: use a sharpie to outline the shape of the field, being careful to exclude any building sites, roads, or other non-planted areas. Step 2: use two separate colors (one for corn, one for beans) to highlight where each crop is planted. Step 3: inside each of these areas, write the crop, total acres and planting date. For the most part in a crop rotation like ours (corn → beans → corn → beans), it should be nearly opposite of what we certified last year, unless we put in a corn-on-corn rotation. Again- should be easy peasy. Well, herein lies the problem.

Tracing field outlines

'14 & '15 Certifications - Same Field

The FSA defines our fields as common land units, or CLUs, using a GIS system that is different than the GPS we use in precision farming. They define a CLU as "an individual contiguous farming parcel, which is the smallest unit of land that has a permanent contiguous boundary, common land cover and land management, a common owner and/or a common producer association". In its simplest form, this sounds much like a farmer would define a field, however the difference is that the FSA designates a field to be "a tract of land separated by permanent boundaries, such as fences, permanent waterways, woodlands, or crop lines that are not subject to change due to

One Producers Story (Anonymous Blog Post) Page 2

farming practices". Translation: their field definitions don't match ours. Again, because this certification is directly tied to future potential crop insurance claims and/or farm program payments, it is important for both parties that we are as accurate as possible.

For example – let's say we certify that in CLU Field 8, 100 acres of corn were planted on 26 May. Later that summer, a severe wind storm comes through and flattens a good portion of our crop, causing it to be totaled out for damages. If only 94 acres were actually planted, then the government pays out way more than they should. But, if 105 acres were actually planted, we (the farmers) are shorted. More importantly, however, accuracy is critical because it directly impacts our APH, or Actual Production History. If you aren't familiar with APH or how it is used in crop insurance, check out the blog "Sign Me Up – The March 15 Deadline Has Passed" I wrote a couple of years ago. *(Disclaimer- while the crop insurance system changed some with the 2014 Farm Bill, the key information remains the same).* Here's how that works: Let's say we planted 100 acres that yielded 200 bushels per acre. That puts this field's APH for this year at 20,000 bushels. But, if we had

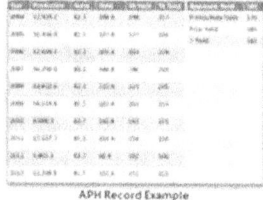
APH Record Example

certified that there were 106 acres planted – and we yielded this same 20,000 bushels... this field's APH would only 188 bushels per acre (20,000/106). When your crop insurance pays out at 80% (or maybe lower) of your APH, you are pretty protective of ensuring it is accurate!!

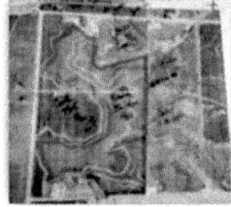
Marking Waterways, Terraces, Etc

What made this experience so painful? Here is just one example...We had a field that our planter monitor said had planted 71.03 acres. The FSA had it as 69.5 acres. Which of us is correct? How can we tell? Here is how it went down: We looked at each of their satellite pictures and noted the size of every terrace, headland and grass waterway (as these weren't planted) so these areas would be taken out of the overall land measurements. You may not be able to tell from the picture, but in tiny print it says 1 = .24 ac waterway, 2= .4 ac headland, 3a and 3b= two parts of a headland around a building totaling .52 ac, and so on. It took 2 of them and 2 of us going over the maps, printouts and the computer system to finally find a 1.89 acre headland that was also indicated as a 1.89 acre crop stand, thus accounting for it twice. One was marked as "9" (which we found on the map) while the other showed up as "H" (that we couldn't find). Once we'd figured that out, it was a pretty easy fix....until we realized we were now off by 5 acres. WHAT? Our "fix" took us in the wrong direction!! Ultimately, we got it straightened out and came within ½ acre of one another. By then, of course, the office was long closed. Thankfully most of our other farms and fields matched pretty closely and we didn't have too much to deliberate on.

At ▇▇▇▇▇ we offer producers Automated Crop Reporting, which makes working with our crop insurance agent much easier and more accurate. They will accept our GPS records as required proof for claims, which can also be submitted electronically. However, with certification, because our GPS differs from the FSA GIS system, they cannot accept our precision records as an accurate means of certification. It is a very manual process (I never expected to be coloring maps on paper) that must be repeated in every county we farm in, every year. I'm sure many of our customers are as thankful as we are that we only farm in 2 counties. Still, even 1-2 certifications can be painful. Imagine having to do this in multiple states!

The CHAIRMAN. Well done, Ms. Casurella.

Mr. Royse, you are recognized for 5 minutes.

STATEMENT OF ROGER ROYSE, J.D., FOUNDER AND OWNER, ROYSE LAW FIRM, PC AND ROYSE AgTech INNOVATION NETWORK, MENLO PARK, CA

Mr. ROYSE. Thank you very much. Thank you for having me here today. I appreciate the opportunity to be at the table and not on the menu, at least for today.

My name is Roger Royse. I am the founder of the Royse Law Firm. We are a Silicon Valley law firm, a full-service firm.

I also founded a group about 5 years ago called Silicon Valley AgTech, which has since morphed into the Royse AgTech Innovation Network. And originally, I founded that group to address the problem that Mr. Tiller pointed out, and that is seeing a lot of very smart technologists in Silicon Valley come up with a lot of cool gadgets that nobody cared about. We have put the technologists together with the farmers, and with the venture capital community, to try to make things happen, and we have been pretty successful at that.

In our law firm, I represent almost all technology startups. A lot of them are what we call ATPs, agriculture technology providers, a few VCs, but for the most part the people that are creating the technology that is being used in the field. And I am here to tell you that we are very interested in anything that will encourage innovation and not hinder it.

I know today that we are going to talk about precision agriculture, especially about data, and it comes down to really three big issues: privacy, security, and ownership. And I hope we have an opportunity to dive into that, because as a lawyer, I can tell you that this definition of *ownership* is a relatively complex thing. It is not as simple as it might seem, especially when we get into data. I have been doing this for 5 years in the agriculture community now, and I have heard all these concerns about all these complex legal provisions that have to be negotiated, to which I reply, "Wel- come to my world." This is the way the rest of the world operates. This is how businesses operate. We negotiate these deals. And I would hope to encourage that Congress take a light hand here when it comes to reshuffling economic decks that have been negotiated by the parties.

Having said that, I applaud these efforts to create standards and to create transparency and certification, but let's keep in mind that not all data is created equal, and all of these agreements will have to be customized to some extent.

Now, a couple of things I do want to mention. We do have some law here. We have section 5 of the FTC Act, which prohibits unfair and deceptive practices. I acknowledge it is not likely to be applied in an agricultural setting. Hopefully, somewhere down the road the USDA may be empowered or enabled to enforce provisions similar to the FTC Act.

I have heard some discussion about applying principles similar to HIPAA and Gramm-Leach-Bliley, which require privacy, disclosure, and security on collectors of data in healthcare and in financial services. Having suffered through Gramm-Leach-Bliley in my practice, I don't think that is appropriate in the agricultural setting.

I do think we can take some instruction from the securities laws. I do a lot of securities financings, and securities is about disclosure. A lot of what we are agonizing over here could be solved with very good disclosure rules.

In sum, again, I hope that Congress treads lightly on this. I hope that other than enabling the USDA to perhaps enforce some standards and remove bad actors from the market, I really hope that we will continue to respect the idea of freedom of contract, as a lawyer, and to allow the market to sort this out, and to let the industry work on these standards.

With that, I am going to cede the rest of my time, and I welcome your questions.

[The prepared statement of Mr. Royse follows:]

PREPARED STATEMENT OF ROGER ROYSE, J.D., FOUNDER AND OWNER, ROYSE LAW FIRM, PC AND ROYSE AGTECH INNOVATION NETWORK, MENLO PARK, CA

Introduction

Thank you for the opportunity to present my testimony and share my view from Silicon Valley and beyond on the AgTech Revolution and the potential role of Congress in its development. My name is Roger Royse. I grew up in western North Dakota, where my family has been (and still is) involved in the produce business since 1948, both in trucking produce from around the country to the Midwest as well as sales of produce to the public. I now reside in northern California and am the founder of the Royse Law Firm, PC, a business law firm based in Silicon Valley with offices in San Francisco and southern California. The Royse Law Firm conducts one of the premier AgTech law practices in the country, helping tech companies with legal transactions including entity formation, financings, commercial contracts, and M&A.

Five years ago, as an adjunct to our AgTech law practice, I started an AgTech group in Silicon Valley. That program has since evolved into the Royse AgTech Innovation Network. Our mandate has been to promote the growing field of AgTech through conferences, events, webinars, white papers, and facilitated meetings between tech companies and the farmers, big Ag and Food, investors, and potential partners. The Network sponsored an accelerator for AgTech companies recently and has taken its message worldwide. I can report that we have been spectacularly successful in our mission, as many of our constituents have launched from our platform, found funding, gained customers, and struck deals with partners. We are on the web at *www.royseAgTech.com* and *www.svAgTech.org*.

I am here today to give you my view of this developing movement that I call the AgTech Revolution, including where it is, where it is going, and how you can help.

Background

American agriculture has undergone several eras of technological innovation. Agriculture was transformed by an industrial revolution through the transition to new manufacturing processes, a green revolution that increased agricultural production worldwide in the latter part of the last century, a genetic revolution that increased crop and livestock production, an information revolution that realized the value of data, and now an AgTech revolution that pushes every acre to its maximum potential. The current AgTech Revolution will be no less significant or sudden than any technological change that has come before it, and Congress has an opportunity to pave the way for this new day by reviewing existing law, considering new incentives and in some cases allowing the market to sort it out.

Numerous factors have enabled the AgTech Revolution, and I summarize a few of them here:

1. *Food Security.* Climate change, a growing global population, rising food prices and environmental pressures are factors that have impacted people's physical, social, and economic access to sufficient, safe, and nutritious food. Such pressures prompted a revolution in the agricultural industry that embraces technological innovation to optimize food safety and production.

2. *The Rise of Consumerism.* The "Grow Local Movement," fueled by the growing middle class' desire for convenience and year-round food, has encouraged development for technologies in urban and vertical farming, waste, transport, and packaging. Additionally, there has been increased consumer support for transparency in the supply chain and GMO and gene editing practices, as well as environmental sustainability.
3. *The Declining Labor Market.* Farm labor shortages and rising wages have resulted in increased labor costs, which then contribute to increased investments in technologies that would replace the manual labor part of the farming process. The average farmworker in California is middle aged, and the problem will get worse before it gets better.
4. *The Changing Agricultural Markets.* A comparison of agricultural production patterns in the U.S. between 1920 and 1995 shows that harvested cropland has declined from 350 to 320 million acres, and the agricultural labor work force has decreased from 26 to just 2.6 percent. In spite of this, agricultural production in 1995 was 3.3 times greater than in 1920 to account for greater demand, demonstrating that productivity has increased and agricultural production methods have changed. Likewise, as the world population has more than doubled between 1950 and 1998, grain production per person has increased by about 12 percent to keep up with the greater world demand.
5. *Increased Rural Internet Connectivity.* The adoption and application of AgTech rests on the availability of the Internet. Due to the accelerating development of AgTech, it is the new rural driver for Internet utilization. As of 2012, about 70% of farms in the U.S. had Internet connectivity.
6. *The Introduction of Venture Capital.* AgTech startups raised more than $320 million this year so far as a result of an uptick in rounds of Series B financings. Funding recipients, equipped with a diverse range of investment themes, are backed by willing and active venture investors who have become more comfortable with this space.
7. *The Rise of Big Data.* Farm data includes site-specific data (*e.g.,* information about seeding rates, soil nutrients, fertilizer, pesticides, water, yield data), meta data (*e.g.,* information about number of acres, inputs applied, crops) and big data (*i.e.,* the aggregation of farm data from numerous operations). Technology now enables farmers to utilize farm data to help inform their work decisions and optimize production.

New Technologies

A list all of the new technologies informing modern agriculture would fill a book, and I do not attempt to list them all here. However, it is worth pointing out a few of the new technologies that I have seen being developed or implemented in the field.

5. *Precision Agriculture.* Precision Ag refers to the suite of hardware and software solutions that allow farmers to optimize efficiencies, reduce inputs, increase production and capture useful data. Precision Ag includes the sensors that gather information, the devices that transmit information, and the software programs that convert the data to actionable information. Sensor tech and the Internet of things (IoT) has gone from merely being able to report information back to the farmer to being able to make recommendations based on that data. The tech can make these recommendations at the level of the individual plant, can deliver that data to a handheld device, and now can even automatically adjust an input to optimize production.

    Many companies have automated the process to a degree previously not thought possible. Self-driving tractors, robotic weeders and thinners, and artificial intelligence (AI) and imaging enabled fruit sorters are in beta or in use. The rise in labor costs have made automation a necessity for farmers, and technology has stepped up to fill the need.
2. *GMO and Gene Editing.* Almost none of our food today is made independent of some form of genetic engineering. A carrot today is a much different plant than a carrot of 100 years ago. The same is true of grains, fruits, and vegetables. The science of genetic engineering has now advanced beyond its original applications, breeding, and GMOs. Recently, genome editing (GEEN) has entered the marketplace. GEEN is a type of genetic engineering in which DNA is inserted, deleted or replaced in the genome using engineered nucleases, or "molecular scissors." GEEN technologies are being developed for both plants and animals that change the food we eat.

3. *Controlled Environment Agriculture.* Controlled environment Ag ("CEA") is also referred to as urban Ag, vertical farming, and indoor Ag. The application of hydroponics, aeroponics, solar tech, LED lighting and advanced building techniques to agriculture has spurred an entire industry designed to grow anything, anywhere at any time. Previously CEA was challenged by high energy costs but advances in technology are making CEA an environmentally friendly solution to many of the world's problems in food production.
4. *Soil Health or Quality.* Soil health (or soil quality) is the capacity of soil to function as an ecosystem that sustains plants, animals, and humans. Many technologies address soil processes to increase productivity, resilience, and environmental quality. Some technologies use biochar or biomass to add nutrients to the soil and some use natural agents to replace insecticides.
5. *Water.* California's recent drought has highlighted the need for water tech. Many of the new technologies are aimed at dealing with the next drought, and take new and innovative approaches. Some of these technologies convert salty or briny water to water that may be used for Ag, through desalination or filtering. Other technologies pull water from air, provide for transport, create water markets to more efficiently distribute water, assist in storage, prevent evaporation, or provide cheap access to groundwater.
6. *Food supply chain.* Having been in the produce business, I have seen in-person the large amount of waste, damage and loss to food from the time it is harvested until it gets to the consumer. Retailers today still rely on methods that existed 50 years ago, but new and developing technologies will monitor produce from field to table so that the ripest product is sold first. E-commerce technologies provide new efficiencies in the shipment and marketing of produce. This is an area where information has real value in preventing losses.

Farm Policy

Today, I would like to propose a few areas where I believe the Federal Government can help agriculture solve the challenges facing it and assist the adoption of new technologies that are designed to help solve some of the problems described above.

1. *Rural Broadband Access.* Broadband access is the key to adoption of AgTech. Farmers and their fields usually have reduced accessibility to high-speed Internet provided by the telephone or cable companies. We need Federal assistance to bring high-speed Internet service to these farms that are located in rural, sparsely-populated areas. Just as 19th century railroads and 20th century interstate highways played leading roles in American prosperity, high-speed Internet is the factor that determines which rural communities, and which farms, will enjoy economic growth and prosperity in the 21st century.

   One way to implement a rural broadband infrastructure is through FirstNet. FirstNet is the largest amount of Federal funding available for broadband infrastructure. Its purpose is to create a national system of emergency communications between all first responders. We propose that Congress ensure that FirstNet emergency communications are provided to rural regions of the U.S. and not limited to making urban population centers a priority like most broadband infrastructure initiatives.

   Alternatively, or contemporaneously, the Federal Government may implement a program that assists and encourages state and local governments to invest in rural broadband infrastructure. Congress can realize such a program by offering states like California a match of Federal resources. This way, from both Federal and state perspectives, the public resources that are invested will be leveraged. Notably, any leveraged public resources under this program would need to be invested in the form of grants in order to actually benefit the unserved and under-served areas of California. Successful funding models include the Internet For All Now Act in California and the broadband infrastructure in the state of New York.

   If we increase access to rural broadband in our nation's rural areas, the same Internet platform used for farming in the fields can be used to increase the overall prosperity and quality of life in our nation's rural communities. For example, broadband-enabled enterprises include health care, education, job training, public safety, and technology. Thus, funding rural broadband infrastructure is the single most promising public resource investment the Federal Government can make to provide unserved and under-served regions of

2. *Specialty Crops in the Farm Bill.* Specialty crops generally consist of plants used by people for food, medicinal purposes, and aesthetic gratification. They are defined by the USDA as "fruits and vegetables, tree nuts, dried fruits, and horticulture and nursery crops (including floriculture)." The diversity of specialty crops and their variety of uses make the task of developing policy in this area particularly challenging. Federal funds can be used to support projects ranging from food safety compliance to distribution systems and marketing.

Federal funds can also provide scientific advances that enable our country to use the most efficient and environmentally sound agriculture technology in the world. Funding this research is imperative due to the industry's increasing reliance on science and technology to maintain profitable production. Likewise, labor dependency is an ongoing concern in the absence of labor saving technology. Federal support for specialty crops still differs in significant ways from commodity crops. Farm bills have historically focused on farm commodity program support for the staple, non-perishable, and generally storable commodities such as corn, soybeans, wheat, cotton, rice, and sugar until specialty crops and organic agriculture were included in a separate title in the 2008 Farm Bill.

Federal investment in agriculture technology is a promising use of farm bill funds to stabilize prices, reduce manual labor, and create permanent jobs with higher income for domestic workers. Thus, adequate funding for the research and development of agriculture technology protects U.S. crop production and keeps producers in business.

3. *Privacy and Data Security in AgTech.* A major issue that farmers are concerned about is whether they have sole ownership of farm data.[1] Because farm data, if kept secret, is information that derives independent economic value from not being publicly known, it could possibly be accorded trade secret protection. Aside from trade secret protection, there are currently no other laws in place to protect the data farmers transfer to AgTech companies.

Existing legislation and regulations regarding privacy and data security are applicable to personal information. In light of the importance of maintaining the security and confidentiality of farm data, Congress might consider legislation to demand accountability and transparency for AgTech Providers ("ATPs") entrusted with managing farm data.

The American Farm Bureau Federation has said that big data can do for agriculture what the Green Revolution and biotechnology did for agriculture. While big data analytics has resulted in improvements in farming, some farmers are concerned that, unless restrictions are imposed on the ATP's use and disclosure of farm data, ATPs might share farm data, including farm research and specialist practices, of one farmer with competing farmers or with third parties, such as environmental and animal welfare lobbies, in a manner disadvantageous to farmers. There is also concern that ATPs might sell farm data to third parties in connection with marketing such third parties' own products and services without compensating farmers for the revenue generated by the ATP from the sale of their farm data.

As a first step towards dealing with these concerns, a coalition of certain farm organizations, including the American Farm Bureau Organization, and certain ATPs, have agreed to a set of non-binding "Privacy and Security Principles for Farm Data" that they hope will be adopted by other ATPs. The complete text of the Privacy and Security Principles for Farm Data is available on the American Farm Bureau Organization's website. It reads very much like privacy and security principles for personally identifiable information, including that the ATP must provide farmers with notice that farm data is being collected and about how the farm data will be disclosed and used. Among other things, it requires that an ATP's collection, access and use of

---

[1] Digital data is data that represents forms of data, including elements of the physical world, by using specific machine language systems that can be interpreted by various technologies (*e.g.,* conversion of a physical scene into a digital image). Digital data collected from farming operations becomes farm data. Farm data includes site-specific data (*e.g.,* information about seeding rates, soil nutrients, fertilizer, pesticides, water, yield data), meta data (*e.g.,* information about number of acres, inputs applied, crops) and big data (*i.e.,* the aggregation of farm data from numerous operations). Farmers can utilize farm data to help inform their work decisions and optimize production.

farm data should be granted only with the affirmative and explicit consent of the farmer and that the ATP will not change the customer's contract without his or her agreement.

The above standards are not law, however, and farmers must prioritize the availability and usability of big data over their own privacy and security. Farmers must also negotiate with data management companies regarding the use of their farm data. There is precedent for Federal regulation of data privacy, although not specifically directed at farming.

The FTC Act (section 5) provides the Federal Trade Commission (the FTC) with broad discretion and authority to regulate data privacy and protection practices of companies across all industries.[2] The FTC imposes sanctions on companies that (i) disclose sensitive information (without consent); (ii) fail to adequately keep consumer's personal information secure; and (iii) fail to follow their own privacy policies.[3]

We suggest that, given the unique nature of agriculture, Congress consider an enforcement regime for farm data that is similar to that granted to the FTC under section 5 the FTC Act.

4. *AgTech Adoption Tax Credits.* Despite the huge advances to be made in agriculture through technology, there are still challenges in its adoption. One of the first problems the Royse AgTech Innovation Network encountered was the disconnect between the technology entrepreneurs and the farmers who would use their tech. There was and is, to be sure, a difference between what technologists think farmers want and what they actually can use, but that gap has been closing as we reach out and involve the grower community in our efforts. The much bigger hurdle is the fact that investing in technology is risky for any business, but especially so for farmers. A grower in California might only have 50 harvests in his lifetime, and cannot gamble a crop on an untested technology. In addition, a grower might be presented with numerous similar technologies. How is he or she to justify the investment in evaluating them all? A partial solution may lie in the Internal Revenue Code of 1986, as amended (the "Code").

The Code currently allows for a research and development credit ("R&D Credit"), which was recently extended by the PATH Act to benefit startups. The R&D Credit is a general business tax credit under Code section 41 for companies that incur research and development (R&D) costs in the United States. While that credit incentivizes development, it does not incentive adoption.

The investment tax credit (ITC), by contrast, allows a taxpayer to deduct part of the cost of installing certain types of energy systems and has been effective in promoting the adoption of solar technology. The ITC, however, is aimed at only a handful of qualifying uses, some of which could be called AgTech. We propose that the ITC be broadened and modified to encourage a wider range of Ag Technologies.

The Royse AgTech Innovation Network is in the process of preparing a white paper on this topic, which will detail how such a credit would work.

Conclusion

Thank you for the opportunity to speak with you today and share my thoughts on the AgTech Revolution, current challenges, and possible solutions. I look forward to taking questions and continuing our dialogue

---

[2] The FTC's primary legal authority to regulate consumer privacy and data security com[e]s from Section 5 of the FTC Act, which prohibits entities from engage in unfair or deceptive acts or practices in interstate commerce. It states in pertinent part: "(1) Unfair methods of competition in or affecting commerce, and unfair or deceptive acts or practices in or affecting commerce, are hereby declared unlawful. (2) The Commission is hereby empowered and directed to prevent persons, partnerships, or corporations, [except certain specified financial and industrial sectors] from using unfair methods of competition in or affecting commerce and unfair or deceptive acts or practices in or affecting commerce."

[3] California has regulations in place regarding privacy and data protection that Congress can adopt and apply to farm data. First, the California Online Privacy Protection Act requires operators of commercial websites and online services (including mobile apps) that collect CA residents' personally identifiable information through a website to conspicuously post their privacy policies. Second, S.B. 1386 (the California Breach Notification Law) requires notification to affected individuals of an unauthorized acquisition of unencrypted computerized data that compromises security, confidentiality, or integrity of personal info of any CA resident. If applied to farm data, the provider of AgTech services would be obligated to notify all farmers whose data had been compromised.

The CHAIRMAN. Well done, Mr. Royse. I appreciate you being here.

The chair would like to remind Members that they will be recognized for questioning in the order of seniority for Members who were here at the start of the hearing. After that, Members will be recognized in order of arrival. I appreciate Members' understanding. I would like to recognize myself for 5 minutes.

Mr. Janzen, I will start with you. You touched on something in your testimony. Farmers have a deep sense of mistrust where data is concerned, the idea of uploading their data into the cloud. And you mentioned that that kind of stems from the fact that there are no laws explicitly protecting that data.

Let me ask you: do you think that an independent verification tool like Ag Data Transparent is sufficient to address the concerns of farmers that they have, or do you think Congress should look into developing data protection standards in the future?

Mr. JANZEN. Thank you.

I think that we are definitely, through the Ag Data Transparency Evaluator, we are filling a gap there, because we are addressing those farmer concerns, that mistrust. If we have widespread participation in the industry, then I feel like we are addressing the farmers' concerns in a way that means that there is no need for any additional legislation that would protect farm data.

Now, if the industry ends up looking the other way and not caring about this, and farmers continue to express mistrust in the future, then it is definitely worth taking another look about whether or not there is something that could be done to improve that situation.

The CHAIRMAN. Mr. Tiller, your thoughts on that?

Mr. TILLER. Well, I actually agree. As I am listening to Todd, I am thinking about what Mr. Royse said. I do think that farmers are astute businessmen. If they will take the time through the knowledge they will gain through things like the Transparency Evaluator, they will make contracts that make sense.

I have always stood for farmers, if they knew what they were bartering. If I am bartering my data for tools, I would never want to take that away from them. Because I know farmers that do understand it, they say: "I don't mind putting my data in an aggregated format, in other words, it be anonymized, my name is off it, to be part of a benchmarking set, when I get something in return." All I can say to end it up is I just want to be careful that I don't, even with the cooperative, in trying to understand ownership and all these issues, I create a world where we can't be innovative, be- cause sometimes innovative does create running out on the bleed- ing edge a little bit. And so that is where I would stand on that. I pretty much agree with Todd.

The CHAIRMAN. Excellent.

Let's talk about actual application of technology and how we can use data in a hands-on way.

Mr. Tiller, Mr. Royse, Texas, California, both of you are having water problems, maybe different kinds of water problems, but water problems. How does big data factor into the better use of irrigation, managing finite water resources?

I will start with you, Mr. Royse.

Mr. ROYSE. Okay. Thanks very much.

We know about water problems out in California. To start, I am seeing a lot of technologies around water that are attacking the problem from ways that are highly innovative and imaginative and sometimes unbelievable.

But with respect to big data, I think that the tools now, the sensors are at the plant level. And we had heard a little bit about precision farming earlier. We are seeing the ability to provide some real conservation through these technology tools, again, highlighting why broadband is so important.

It is important to note, by the way, that the technology has moved, that I have seen, to where each sensor is its own Internet user. In other words, it is not like a Christmas tree. It is not daisy-chained. Each sensor has to load up to the cloud. That requires a tremendous amount of Internet access. But through these sensors and through being able to provide just the right amount of water in the right place at the right rate, we are seeing data being used to reduce water usage and address our drought problem.

The CHAIRMAN. Thank you.

Mr. Tiller.

Mr. TILLER. I would add a couple things there. I am in total agreement with what he is bringing up. But I spent a decade also as an ag lender, so profitability is everything in the end.

What I would say is, it is about water use, but I can see farmers understanding profitability better and even changing crops, growing different things, being able to use their water in different ways, if they had the data to help them understand what is the most profitable crop on this piece of ground.

Maybe I don't have a full pivot or circle of cotton. Maybe that 130 is now 60. What do I do with the other 70 acres? Those sorts of things data can help you understand.

The CHAIRMAN. Thank you.

I now recognize Ranking Member Nolan for 5 minutes.

Mr. NOLAN. Thank you, Mr. Chairman.

I have just got one question, then I will yield to my colleagues here, and it is this: As ag data improves and has become more useful to farmers, there appears to be a widening gap among farmers, as well, that have access to this technology and those who don't. And oftentimes some of the best producers in the world are a mile or two apart from one another as opposed to downtown where every 50 feet there is a user. It makes it a little easier financially for businesses to provide those services.

To be sure, as these technologies continue to grow, those who have access to it will grow and prosper and those who don't will suffer, even though they may very well be among our greatest producers.

How do you expect the cost of getting these technologies to all the farmers, how do you expect those costs to go down? And what ideas or suggestions do you have for us to consider for getting those costs down to an affordable level where all of our farm producers will have access to them? Thank you.

Whoever. Step up. Tell us what you think.

Mr. TILLER. I will share a few thoughts, but I want to make sure I leave time for the other panel members.

That is a vision of the cooperative, right? I mean, that is what we would be about, making sure all producers had access to the technologies that are developed in a fair and reasonable cost mechanism. Some of the price points of some of the best tools have been too high, but I have news for you, the adoption of those has been very low. It looks like there has been adoption, but even among some of the biggest growers, not what you would think. They are going to have to bring the price point down to prove the value even there.

I would say I really think innovation and technology and broadband is actually going to be very helpful for a grower with 100 acres. He is going to be able to store data in ways he never could before because of the mobility of the smartphone, being able to carry that computer in his pocket. It takes so little cost of equipment to actually go out and implement these things. And these are very scalable technologies.

I almost see it going the other way. Every grower will have access to tools to make decisions in ways they have never had it before.

I think these sensors are going to get so cheap. I was looking at some Bluetooth technology that the sensor was $11, and you could utilize these. That is an example. I actually think it will go the other way.

I will yield to the other panelists.

Mr. NOLAN. Real quick like, however, it is apparent that some of the companies look at this and they say: Well, I have a customer every 1½ mile, 2 miles, I am not going to invest in that. And they are not investing in it in many cases.

You are right, the technology will lower the cost and increase the benefits and whatnot, but if you don't have the technology, how do we make sure we get it to everyone?

Mr. TILLER. What are you calling technology? I am going to tell you——

Mr. NOLAN. Broadband is what I am talking about.

Mr. TILLER. Okay. Now, there you go. I am in total agreement with you there. Most of the farmers, I am amazed, even with age, carrying the smartphone. I have seen this happen. Four years ago I could be in a meeting and you could carry it on. It doesn't matter what the age group, I can't carry on the meeting unless I ask them: Can we all silence our phones? I never thought that would be an issue because of the average age of the farmer.

We have it. But you are right, connecting that and being able to stay connected, it is a criteria we really are going to have a gap to feed the world. If we don't close that gap by providing that infrastructure, that is something that is going to be missing.

Yes, I do agree with that. That is kind of a third-party touch to the things I talk about. I don't develop that, but I have to have it. Mr.

NOLAN. Do you see an investment by the Federal Government in broadband expansion and infrastructure as being something we should consider?

Mr. TILLER. What has driven out the rural growth of telecommunications all this time has been the support of the RUS, the Universal Service Fund, and that mentality. I don't know why we can't keep doing what we are doing.

I was involved with telecommunications for over 20 years, served on a cooperative telecommunications board. Some of the RUS permitting that is required to get the loan that you have to do even before the loan is ready to be made and the cost involved, if some of that could be looked at, it would be much easier to get there. There are a lot of things that you guys could do from the Committee to actually help build that out. You could be the catalyst to really keep that moving.

Mr. NOLAN. Thank you.

Mr. Chairman, my time is up. Thank you, Mr. Chairman.

The CHAIRMAN. Hey, listen, I was watching the clock there. I didn't want to cut you off.

Mr. Abraham, you are recognized for 5 minutes.

Mr. ABRAHAM. Thank you, Mr. Chairman.

Mr. Royse, what are the protections in the agricultural sector for data, and how do they compare to other businesses as far as protection of data?

Mr. ROYSE. Yes, so it is commonly said that there really is no law of farm data. There are general rules around data. There is no Federal law of farm data at this point. In California, where I am from, we have state law that protects the privacy of what we call personally identifiable information, which could apply to farm data. It doesn't always.

But most of the time, farmers are going to have to rely on the law of trade secrets. And as you know, we now have a Federal trade secret law. But trade secret is a little tricky. It is not automatic for farm data. The information has to be proprietary, has to be valuable, has to be secret, and the owner has to take steps to keep it secret. It is very easy for somebody to lose trade secret protection for this data.

The way that it is commonly protected these days is through contract, I mean, and that is why we are having a lot of these discussions, is because these contracts can be relatively complex and involved.

Mr. ABRAHAM. Thank you.

Mr. Tiller, you said in your testimony, your written testimony, which I actually read, that all growers will be impacted by the information revolution, and I totally agree with that. We grow more cotton on my farm this year than we have grown in the last 10 years.

What will be the biggest impact of those farmers that don't invest in the information revolution?

Mr. TILLER. It is just very difficult to compete. I have never liked to think of myself as competing against my neighbor, because I am competing in a world market. Cotton price, it is a global economy. But in truth, as I do, there is a limited amount of land, and growers are trying to rent that land. The most efficient producer is going to do the best job of creating the yield off that farm.

I think that the benchmarking that is there today, if we are not using data, just look at the varieties. Look at what has happened in cotton, as an example, in the last 10 years. I am amazed. I do cringe when I pay some of these technology fees, but, in truth, I have the best varieties I have ever had.

Now, do they compensate for the difference in a $100 bag of seed and a $400? It is difficult. I did the math this year in a very rough cotton year, and I am questioning about what I have in the field. But if we don't continue to understand and be able to relate to those varieties and understand I should put this variety on this soil and these water conditions, I mean, I am not going to be as profitable as I can, and then I will be not as self-sustaining.

Data helps us be more self-sustaining, so I can look to myself to help myself be shored up. And I can look to insurance when I have weather-related events that I have no control over, but I can control what variety I have in the field. That is an example.

Mr. ABRAHAM. I mean, knowledge is power and knowledge is money in the farming community. Thank you.

Mr. Chairman, I yield back.

The CHAIRMAN. The gentleman yields back.

I recognize Mrs. Bustos, for 5 minutes.

Mrs. BUSTOS. Thank you, Mr. Chairman.

And thanks for our panel members for being here today.

Mr. Royse, your testimony, which I read in advance, was one of the most fascinating agricultural pieces of information that I have read in a very long time. But, it is a very impressive group of people here. Thank you so much.

My district starts in central Illinois and covers the entire northwestern part of the State of Illinois. Ag is our number one economic driver. I am very, very interested in what you are talking about today.

I want to tell you a really quick story. We have a brand new company that started in a town called Galesburg. It is called Integrated Precision Agriculture. And what they have done is they have taken unmanned aerial vehicles, and they are using that for spraying and surveying crops.

But what happened was they go to the state's Department of Agriculture and they encountered this issue where the state's Department of Agriculture struggled to understand the business needs. And so they pointed out that in order to get their pesticide license, they didn't know if they were sure of what kind of training they needed. Did they need ground training or did they need aerial training?

And so I just bring that up to say there are some struggles here with new technology and how we are going to move forward. But, it is a story that illustrates that what do we need to deal with in government. My question really is aimed at all of you, maybe a couple questions.

With regard to data and analytics, how can the Federal Government not only remain flexible, but also help usher in new technology? That is question number one. Is there a role for the USDA staff on the ground, or our university extension programs?

Anybody can take that first. Nobody needs to repeat what the person ahead of them said. But whoever would like to address that first and then we will just kind of go through the list.

And you have an Illinois connection, right?

Ms. CASURELLA. I grew up in Illinois.

Mrs. BUSTOS. Then you go first.

Ms. CASURELLA. All right. I will take that. I moved out of Illinois when I was 16, though.

Mrs. BUSTOS. Okay, then you get moved. Go ahead. You are all right.

Ms. CASURELLA. In terms of ag data and analytics and how the USDA can provide a role, a big part of it is providing best management practices for farmers. And I will use an example that impacts the Central Sands of Wisconsin as well as northern Illinois.

With potatoes grown in sandy soil, they are typically irrigated. And if you use the data collected on a combination of sensors, it is sensors that understand the nitrates coming through the soil to know when you need to apply your fertilizer, your pesticide. If you apply it right after or right before a rain, it is going to go right down through to the place, it is not going to affect the top 8″ in water growth.

County extension and county offices, specifically on the NRCS side, can definitely help farmers understand data, available options, and what farming practices they need to use. And I will couple that with add EQIP dollars to, in the case of irrigated potatoes in sandy soils, add EQIP dollars to help the producer pay for what could be a $50,000 investment in technology. But for potatoes, if you manage them correctly, your N_2 stores go from eight truckloads to one truckload if you manage irrigation.

There are a whole lot of benefits if there is the right research study and best practices that a farmer can use, plus funding, to help him get that technology in place. That is one example.

Mrs. BUSTOS. Thank you.

Anybody else have anything to add?

Mr. ROYSE. I do. It is an interesting thing from the standpoint of the tech providers that I work with, is they are always very surprised—that example you just gave, I have a hundred like that—to find out just how highly regulated agriculture is. And we run into walls all the time. We run into business models and business plans that just don't work because of that.

I love the idea of education. It would be nice to see some coordination possibly, but I don't know that I have any answers other than that, but to say that you put your finger on what is a real issue in this area and something that, I don't know if I would say it is stifling innovation, but it is one of those challenges we have to work through.

Mr. TILLER. I want to make one last statement. You did mention the extension and the land-grant universities, and I am going to tell you, when I first started farming 35 years ago, they were unbelievably relevant; and they still are relevant, because they are the only agnostic view we may get.

I think that digital agriculture will give them a new way to actually make their data visible. And so I am hoping that they can embrace that. They may need funding to do that.

But I know it will be helpful, because they are not selling me anything. And to have them give me a view of the seed varieties or the secret recipes I should be using *versus* me trying to decide or have some company selling me something trying to tell me. I would definitely like you all to continue in that realm too.

Mrs. BUSTOS. That is a great point.

And with that, I am out of time. Thank you very much.

The CHAIRMAN. The gentlelady yields back.

And I recognize the gentleman from Nebraska for 5 minutes.

Mr. BACON. Thank you very much, Mr. Chairman.

I appreciate you all coming in today and sharing your expertise and your testimony.

Some of the questions I have you have touched on a little bit, but I just want to make sure I understand it. But before I do, since I was raised on a farm, we raised corn and soybeans, beef cattle, until I was 21, then I joined the Air Force for 30 years, and that transformation over that 30 years is just incredible.

When I was 20 years old driving on a tractor discing, my main concern was finding an AM radio station and trying to find a good baseball game for something to keep me amused. Today we have GPS on almost every piece of equipment. Our combines are pumping out maintenance data all over, yield data. Our irrigation systems know what part of the fields need more concentration than others.

I was just at a ranch with 75,000 head of cattle. Every trough was computerized, every water tank, and based on the age of the cattle, different blends of feed. It was mainly computerized. Every head of cattle they had to analyze, so to maximize the output for each head of cattle.

I just find it incredible where we have gone. I clearly see a need for broadband and big data. And I have seen different estimates what it is going to cost to fully put this out in our rural communities.

Do any of you have a good estimate of what it will cost in the end to really do a rural broadband system for our country? A big question. What is the cost? Has anyone seen a good estimate?

Mr. TILLER. I do want to say this. I wouldn't tackle that one, but back in the day when I was sitting on a telecommunication board when Internet was new, we took a poll of the board. We said: "Who is going to want this?" And I can remember some of the older guys on the board: "Nobody." And I was one of the guys who said: "Well, I want it." We thought out of the 1,800 alliance subscribers that maybe 100 would want it. Look what happened today, they all want it. And they don't want what? They don't want that little pipe carrying 2,400 baud, they want a big pipe.

What it is going to cost today it is hard to say, because technology is going to keep wanting more. It is going to have to feed the beast. But if we want to be effective, efficient, and productive, we have to do that. I don't know the cost, but I know it is necessary.

Mr. BACON. I just think it is probably good to start big picture. What is the cost to get broadband out there, and then we could strategize how to get there.

Now, you touched on this a little bit. What can we do in the farm bill to make some progress there? You touched on it a little bit, but I just want to make sure we have clarity. Is there a way to partner with states and local governments and private industry? Because obviously people are going to make money on this as well, so it shouldn't be totally a Federal cost. But any thoughts on that? And

I just open it up to the floor, because I am earnestly seeking answers here.

Mr. JANZEN. Perhaps grants to State Departments of Agriculture. I know, like in Indiana, we always hear about rural broadband and the need for that. And perhaps with some incentive money in a future farm bill, that would be enough to push those states to invest.

Mr. BACON. Incentives.

Mr. JANZEN. Yes. And I don't know the cost either of what this would be to make America's farms connected. But I have to think, when you look back in history, every major investment we have made in rural infrastructure has paid dividends for generations, rural water, rural electric, roads. I think this is the next big one. Mr.

BACON. If we get the broadband put out, I don't foresee that changing as much. The applications riding within it will change, clearly. If you get the infrastructure in getting to your point, Mr. Tiller, that the applications within it will change. But we need to get the infrastructure in place. I am just trying to figure out the best way to do it. I don't know if it is strictly a private endeavor or if there is a partnership there. I think there should be probably some kind of partnership.

Mr. TILLER. The USF fund, that has been a private-public partnership all this time. I remember back in the day, I was on a farm board from 1986 really up to 2004. It is needed. I mean, that is that private-public partnership that goes on to make those things work.

Bringing lending in different ways, through RUS, through the different funding mechanisms, that is the way you do it. I don't think the government would just go out and say: "How do we take that?" It would be these private partnerships.

Mr. BACON. I will just close. When I get feedback going around, I am from the Omaha district, so I have a county and a half, more urban than suburban. We have some farms on the west and north side and southwest and so forth. But we have a huge agri-industry, a lot of processing commodities and, I mean, transportation.

But I get out a lot in Nebraska to learn on this, and the first issue is affordable crop insurance, I hear it all over. Second, foot-and-mouth disease concerns, what would happen, having an insurance plan there. Infrastructure, which is tied to broadband, is probably the fourth issue I hear. I think that is a common thing I hear.

Anyway, thank you for your time.

Mr. Chairman, I yield back.

The CHAIRMAN. The gentleman yields back.

Ms. Plaskett, you are recognized for 5 minutes.

Ms. PLASKETT. Thank you so much, Mr. Chairman.

And thank you all for being here.

I wanted to ask a couple of questions. We have had a really good discussion on both sides of the aisle about this issue, really coming at this in a bipartisan manner in how we can address the issues of broadband in rural areas.

It is interesting, because yesterday the Committee held a hearing about innovations in the specialty crop industry, but much of the discussion today is around commodity crops. And so one of the questions I have, and this is to any of the witnesses, how can technologies that you work with help fruit and vegetable growers? And are there unique benefits of data technology and the discussion we have about increased broadband technology for specialty crops?

Mr. ROYSE. I would like to just offer, one of the comments one of the panelists made, it is very true, is these technologies really do translate. And we see a lot of tech that originates in California in the specialty crop area, and almost immediately it is across the country. It is out in the commodity crops.

In a way my viewpoint is that these are technologies that are going to be useful across a lot of different crops, especially the data.

Ms. CASURELLA. What I would add to that is production agriculture, your row crops, is very different than your fruits, nuts, and trees in terms of how I would apply technology. If I were looking at fruits, nuts, and trees, I would focus more on your aerial imagery. I mean, the technology is such that you can count the number of tomato plants in a field very accurately using the automation, whether it is 3 to 5 meter imagery or drones.

The application of technology will vary, depending on the crops, but I also agree you can try to cross. But you are not going to put a tractor in an area where you are counting your trees and your fruit on those trees.

Aerial imagery and some of those kinds of things are far more expensive than the production agriculture, but there are a lot of pretty neat things that are happening, I will call it, in garages and homes and those kinds of things, but not a lot that, as Billy said, is good for mainstream specialty growers.

Ms. PLASKETT. I know that you were talking before about fertilizer and the time in which to put that. I think that, for specialty crop growers, that is an issue as well.

In the Virgin Islands we go from drought to heavy rains. And having technology to help the farmer support irrigation issues, which are really important for them, and how to regulate that would be something that this technology would be supportive of as well.

Ms. CASURELLA. Yes. And there, you may want to start with sensors, soil sensors, and moisture flow as a pretty simple Internet-connected device to collect a lot of data.

Ms. PLASKETT. I know that our extension, the University of the Virgin Islands, the extension is doing a lot in terms of sensors. But the technology probably isn't going to come from the extension. It is going to come from other high-tech places and then being able to apply those or something that would be really helpful.

My other question is for Mr. Tiller. We were talking about cooperatives. You noted that cooperatives are trying methods for farmers to come together to find greater market power, and you have been doing some work with farmers to do this in the ag data market.

Could you explain how the Grower Information Service Cooperative is positioned to draw value for farmer members, and how would patronage return be generated from aggregated farm data? Mr. TILLER. That is a good question, and the reason it is a good question is today it hasn't been done. I always tell growers, let's be simple. Let's start out with what I call collect and store. Let's don't get too far down the road, because until we get the data into place where we can do something with it. Because I always sort of chuckle when this farm group says: "We are doing all this stuff with data." And I always say: "What data?" They probably don't have much data, because it has been very difficult to bring in and collect.

We want to use the platform initially so farmers would have a place to store that data. And then they could begin to share that with their agronomist, with people that work with their data, not looking at big data initially, doing simple things to create small data that would be actionable for their farms.

An example would be in the vegetable industry, *et cetera,* we want to work there and here is why. I have groups from all over the world that call me about this data cooperative. And I have said: "I can't see why we can't franchise this same idea, same platform, to create data communities. Because if you only have 80 or 90 growers, you don't really want to set up a cooperative, wherever that is at, and try to get into all the technicalities and the cost, but set up a data community." And we are trying to work with some groups right now of how that might look and be managed, managed on a similar platform to ours.

So today I would say collect, store, but we have to analyze. Stored data is not worth anything to the farmer if we don't make a decision with it. I have sort of reached a point where sometimes in the industry there are groups that say: "Really, we don't want it shared outside of here because we don't really want anything else done with it." That doesn't work for a grower. I have to be able to make decisions with that data.

Ms. PLASKETT. Thank you.

Thank you, Mr. Chairman.

The CHAIRMAN. The gentlelady yields back.

The gentleman from Ohio, Mr. Gibbs, is recognized for 5 minutes.

Mr. GIBBS. Thank you, Mr. Chairman.

First, I would make a couple of comments on broadband, the need in the rural area, absolutely, definitely. I don't know if that means, broadband means more fiber, more cell towers, I don't know how that interrelates.

But I can tell you, working with one of my local companies in my district, fiber has come down, is cheaper now than coaxial cable. And this cable company, it is a privately owned company in several of my counties, is running fiber to every residence on their customer base. And the technology, how it all works, I had an interesting morning that day, I learned a lot.

But I wanted to know, Mr. Tiller, your cooperative that you started, you say you have 1,400 members, when Mr. Royse talks about privacy, security, and ownership, what are your cooperative rules? How do you handle it? Because you would be like the miniature scale compared to nationally.

Mr. TILLER. Well, we are still learning, but that is why I am so staunch about this. I appreciated Mr. Royse's comments that ownership is a complex issue. But when I am talking to a grower, they want to know that their data is within the contractual rights of the co-op they own the data that is placed in there. They could be part of aggregated data sets and they would be anonymized. But they would own that data. They could take their data at any point.

Mr. GIBBS. What was that?

Mr. TILLER. They could take their the data, it is portable. They would move it.

Now, what could they do with it? That is the problem today. A lot of groups tell us: "You can take your data. But if you can't do anything with it when you leave, and you really can't take it in a format that you can really put it into something else, you haven't left with a lot."

The beauty of this is, this is just a group of growers deciding what they want to do. If other growers want to join in that effort along those rules of understanding that; it is an evolving thing. Where we are at today won't be where we are at in 2 or 3 years. I believe we will have data sets that will be valuable to growers around benchmarking within the next 2 to 3 years.

Mr. GIBBS. And your 1,400 members, I am kind of assuming they are all different levels of capabilities.

Mr. TILLER. They are all different crops, all different levels.

Mr. GIBBS. Levels being able to collect data and how they are using the data, right?

Mr. TILLER. Yes. I have farmers that joined the co-op that literally, they might have one tractor on their farm out of five that are using GPS. And I have asked them in the conversation, "What made you want to join the co-op?" Even some that don't even have that. And they are looking for the co-op to even be an educational force for them.

I don't know what to do around data. We have always solved problems in ag, kind of joining together. There was a thought around that. We have had members join at that level.

And then I wish the gentleman from Nebraska was still here. One of my most astute growers, Roric Paulman, out of Nebraska, I mean, this guy employs more technology. I learn more about how to employ technology when I go to his farm than anyplace I have ever seen. My example is, you are right, it is a spectrum. But it is all crops, too.

Mr. GIBBS. Now, kind of an another thought. Data is collected, and let's say it is flying pesticide, herbicides, or fertilizer, whatever. What are your thoughts about a government agency being able to come in? For one aspect, a producer could use as protection: I have the actual records here, blah, blah, blah. But the other side, say the EPA or whatever. Has that conversation ever come up?

Mr. TILLER. That conversation comes up a lot. You are from Ohio, you may know John Fulton, Ohio State. Those are conversations we have had with him because he is academia, doing research, taking grant money. I am very concerned that when there is grant money involved it might be FOIAble. And a grower might not want that data out there. Not doing anything wrong, just wants his privacy looked at in that way.

At the co-op we think about that. We have never looked to take grants or bring in any dollars like that, we have used private money to fund us, because we do want to be a separate database owned by growers where they own this individually.

Mr. GIBBS. That is one aspect, from that aspect. I am thinking about another aspect of being able to come in and, I guess, subpoena you, or a search warrant.

Mr. TILLER. Well, I guess that can happen. Let's use some examples of things that are out in the tech industry like Box, Dropbox, these places that store data. If that could happen to us, it could happen to them.

I think that is a much larger issue than in ag because we have tried to remain totally separate and private for those very reasons. We have had growers concerned about that, to be honest. I mean, what would keep EPA from wanting to just subpoena my records around if I am in a watershed and if we stored them there.

And those are things that we are trying to work through now as we talk to growers, so there is a lot of caution being put there. But at the same time there is so much to be garnered when farmer's data are controlled and understanding that data so we can do the right things. We are good stewards of the land.

Mr. GIBBS. I agree with that. It is a question of we have to be able to answer some of these questions so farmers have more confidence to do this.

I yield back.

The CHAIRMAN. The gentlemen yields.

Mr. Dunn is recognized for 5 minutes.

Mr. DUNN. Thank you very much, Mr. Chairman.

Let me start by saying, I am not a framer, unlike General Bacon, who was sitting here to my right, and I didn't grow up on a farm. And I am fascinated by the sheer penetrance of information technology on today's farms. You hear about rural broadband, and you think: Oh, people want TV out in the small towns, too. No, that is not what they are talking about.

I am really, really impressed. We have a very agrarian district, a lot of farmers, 300 miles across. It is the number one economic activity in my district. And I am learning a lot about farming very quickly.

Let me ask, Mr. Tiller, I will start with you, first question. There are large swaths of my district that do not have broadband. What happened to these farmers who just at this point in time, and maybe going forward for a while, don't have access to broadband?

Mr. TILLER. There are ways to collect data without broadband. You can actually store it on the phone, sync it later.

Mr. DUNN. Walk the fields.

Mr. TILLER. That is right. You do exactly what you have been doing. But my whole point, that is why we have to get there.

Mr. DUNN. But they can't compete as well, and they like to export, too. There are some pretty big farms.

Mr. TILLER. That is right. It is something you need to address. I mean, I am speaking for those farmers. I know they want better access to the technology of broadband. It is that simple.

Mr. DUNN. I have spent a fair amount of time in the space launch programs, and I can tell you they want to put a lot of low Earth orbit satellites out there that they say will cover these areas. I don't know. I also spent a lot of time trying to get fiber out there. In fact, one of our space launch consortiums was making fiber in space for telecoms and then sending it back to Earth to plant in the ground. It is a confusing world.

I do want to address the gentleman from Ohio's question about privacy of data, though. I think that that is really interesting. We get it that you can own your data, but your data has already been shared with some big growers consortium perhaps, or not, or not. But is your data private from, let's just say, the IRS?

Mr. TILLER. Well, it is at this point. You would know that better than me. I mean, you all are making the rules. At this point I haven't had those——

Mr. DUNN. That is a rule that would interest you?

Mr. TILLER. That is where I am going to rely on you all to actually not protect just the farmers, you are going to want to protect everyone from those sorts of concerns.

Mr. DUNN. But what are the privacy issues in agriculture, the secret issues? Are there secret competition issues?

Mr. TILLER. That is never really the concern. Farmers, right now they are not even putting the data in a warehouse where it could be used.

And I find that privacy is a concern. For most of them it is not the greatest concern. They want to know: If I want to share it, who can I share it with? They want to make sure they control those aspects. We are trying to really build a platform where they will have that control.

The main concern farmers have is: How easily can I get it there? What value do I really have once it is there? Is there anything that can be done with it? Those are things that are important today, they weren't as important 5 years ago, but today that is the question. Most of them because they have seen all the social media, how things go, so they are more comfortable around data. But they want to know what value. If I put effort and time and money, what do I garner when I get to the end of the day?

Mr. DUNN. I will say, in closing, that no conversation with a farmer in my district ends without some comment about access to broadband. And that, of course, is much more acute out in the farm country. And we want to be sure we address that in the farm bill, and we want to be sure that you help us address it properly.

With that, Mr. Chairman, I yield back. Thank you.

The CHAIRMAN. Thank you.

And I recognize the gentlelady from Delaware for 5 minutes.

Ms. BLUNT ROCHESTER. Thank you. And excuse me for having to step out for a moment.

This issue is one that is probably really important and exciting to me, especially in my home State of Delaware. I had an opportunity to go around with some of our farmers and use some of their technology and see what is happening. And so hopefully my questions that I am interested in haven't already been asked.

But one of the things that I was interested in is, I heard as I walked in about the issue of broadband, and right now there seems to be, just like in the past with the digital divide, you have sometimes those who get access to new technologies and others who don't.

I am curious about whether you think the cost of some of this technology, when we can expect to see it become more available to a broader group of individuals, whether they are farmers that have great big companies *versus* the family farmer. Can you talk a little bit about accessibility and kind of bridging that divide?

Mr. ROYSE. I will jump in just for a minute on one part of this. And that is, I am seeing that the cost of the devices is going down tremendously over the last 5 years. It is becoming very affordable and accessible.

And you are absolutely right, cost is a very big issue with farms, a lot of which are very low margin businesses. And cost was a gating factor early on. But, that problem is being solved, at least at the device level, with regard to the Federal cost. The government cost of building the superhighways and the access, that I don't know.

Mr. JANZEN. I wanted to add that we are still at a place where farmers are trying to sort out what is the return on investment when they upload their data to all these cloud-based platforms. Right now most farmers are still paying to store their data in the cloud.

But, the long-term hope is that eventually that value proposition flips and we start to see farmers getting paid to upload their data, because the companies are getting so much value out of that, that it is worth returning some of that investment back to farmers. And so that will bring the costs of these services down for farmers as well.

Ms. BLUNT ROCHESTER. Got you.

When you gave your testimony earlier, I heard different things about trust, about fear, some of the different concerns about who owns the data. And I guess my question would be, we have seen that the technology has been growing, but we have also heard some of the challenges.

Can you each identify what you would say is the one major concern that you have in making use of the new technologies? If you had just one thing that really is that major concern, what would it be?

And we can start with Mr. Royse.

Mr. ROYSE. Well, okay. I would like to come back to the privacy issue, because I want you to imagine a scenario where somebody walks into my office and they say: "I have this new technology. It is going to sit on a drone and it is going to gather yield data of a farm." Or maybe financially, I am going to figure out how profitable that farm is.

And then I am going the take that data and I am going to go sell it to the companies that sell the inputs to the farm because they know how profitable the farm is. And by the way, in California a lot of the farm land is leased. Maybe I will go sell it to one of that farmer's neighbors so he can come and he knows what that farm is worth. Or maybe I will sell it back to the owner of the land.

I think there really is a privacy issue here. Now, we deal with that, of course, through contracts, and in California we have this concept of personally identifiable information. But when I hear about trust issues, that is kind of the first thing I think about. It is not the only thing, but it is the first thing I think about.

Ms. BLUNT ROCHESTER. I have 50 seconds.

Ms. CASURELLA. Yes. What growers are most concerned with producers are two things. One is if they use their precision ag data, the data collected on their tractor for reporting, is the government going to get more than the government is supposed to get?

What is on that card, what is in that data could be their seed planted in the ground and an as-applied fertilizer application. They only want to share the seed, they don't want to share the variety and the type. If it is corn and it is planted on this field with this parameter, they are happy to share that because it is required. They don't want anything else to go.

The challenge is, how do you enable the use of the data without disclosing more than is required?

Ms. BLUNT ROCHESTER. Thank you.

Nine seconds.

Mr. JANZEN. My big concern is that farmers understand the contracts they are signing up for.

Ms. BLUNT ROCHESTER. Got you. Thank you.

Mr. TILLER. I would just reiterate, collaboration of all the things we have talked about, going back to when Mr. Royse was talking about literally even the drones. Let's take it from there even to the data level. If I shared data like Todd is talking about with a third-party company, do I understand what is going to happen to that data? Is it going to stay there? Are they going to share it with affiliates? Are those affiliates going to try to sell things to me based on what they learned?

Ms. BLUNT ROCHESTER. Thank you. My time has expired.

The CHAIRMAN. The gentlelady's time has expired.

I recognize the gentleman from Georgia for 5 minutes.

Mr. ALLEN. Thank you, Chairman.

And thank you for sharing with us.

Obviously, technology is critical to the continued operation of our farming industry. And, of course, we have made tremendous strides. And, of course, you all have been a part of that and I appreciate all your efforts in making these things work.

We are working through the farm bill, the next farm bill. And in the 2014 Farm Bill, it was clear that USDA should allow producers or an agent of a producer to report data, including geospatial data, electronically or conventionally, to the Department. This provision was designed to reduce the administrative burdens and costs for producers.

Ms. Casurella, do you have some insight on why this is not being done?

Ms. CASURELLA. I am not even sure where to start. First, it is the——

Mr. ALLEN. Well, we have 3 minutes and 55 seconds.

Ms. CASURELLA. Okay. First, it is the uncertainty; well, no, first, the farmer doesn't even know it is happening to them. If you are going into the FSA or you are going to your crop insurance agent and the FSA sends the data, the crop insurance—and the crop insurance data through their crop insurance company sends the data to the FSA, the producer doesn't know it is happening.

They also don't know it is incomplete data. And the whole farming industry is conditioned to have data match. When they go into the FSA county office and they get their form 578 and they report 32.78 acres, that equals their CLU. And then they go into their crop insurance acres and report 31.2 acres of insurable acres for their crop insurance.

If there is a GAO audit or a compliance or a claim, what are valid acres? Is it the acres that they reported in crop insurance, that are probably the acres that they planted in the field, or the acres that they certified in FSA? I mean, there are still so much confusion on the impact to a farmer, the impact on the FSA program.

If I report accurately, do my base acres change? Well, not in this farm bill. But will they in the next one?

Mr. ALLEN. That is why we are talking about it. Again, we are working on the next farm bill.

Ms. CASURELLA. Yes.

Mr. ALLEN. And we need to get this solved.

Do you or any of the panel have any idea how we can solve this issue?

Ms. CASURELLA. I will say one thing. Let the farmers plant the acres they plant. Let the farmers report the acres they plant. It doesn't have to be farm tract field. It doesn't have to be common land unit. And let the government figure out then, if I plant a boundary and it covers 3 CLUs or within 1 CLU, come up with the rules for how to handle that data.

But don't make the government report with boundaries that are set anywhere from 5 to 25 years ago that maximize producer benefits. Let the farmers report what they report, and give the agency the dollars to be able to adapt the program to collect actual data.

Mr. ALLEN. Okay. Thank you so much for your feedback.

Any other comments regarding that problem from the other members.

All right. I have just a minute. It is my understanding that the NRCS, which is the Natural Resources Conservation Service within the USDA, is coordinating well with the 3D Elevation Program, or 3DEP. And my question is to everyone on this panel. How can USDA best leverage elevation data via these standard mapping technologies, such as LiDAR, to maximize farm management decisions? Does it go back to this same issue?

Mr. TILLER. You were saying elevations.

Mr. ALLEN. Right.

Mr. TILLER. Repeat the question. I had trouble hearing you.

Mr. ALLEN. It is where the NRCS service within the USDA is coordinating with the 3D Elevation Program within the U.S. Geological Survey in the Department of the Interior—in short, 3DEP is the nationwide LiDAR, L-i-D-A-R Program, in its enhanced elevation data. And my question is, how can the USDA best leverage that elevation data to make it available?

Mr. TILLER. Well, to make it available, maybe that could be a public data set. I would love to be able to pull that in to have that elevation data. As tractors are going through the field with the GPS on them, we get elevation data, too.

Mr. ALLEN. Okay.

Mr. TILLER. With that elevation data, you could actually do a lot to really check where you are at. Deb or one of the others might have a better feel for it. I don't really know the value yet. There are people around me that might. I don't feel like I could really get—

Mr. ALLEN. Well, that is the concern that has been voiced to my office. I think it goes back with trying to solve this in the next farm bill.

And, Mr. Chairman, I am out of time, I yield back. Thank you so much.

The CHAIRMAN. The gentleman yields.

The gentleman from Florida is recognized for 5 minutes.

Mr. LAWSON. Mr. Chairman, thank you for the opportunity.

The biggest problem that I have is the way it happened in Congress is trying to do two or three meetings at the same time and read on my way coming here. I want to thank the Committee.

I want to thank you all for being here. And I know that you already discussed the issue regarding the lack of broadband.

But my question is different. Here in north Florida there is the issue with the lack of rural broadband and access. Can you elaborate on how the lack of rural broadband hinders the implementation of telematics among farmers and regions? Can anyone?

Mr. TILLER. I would just reiterate for you, what it is boiling down to is this. Everything that is out there that really is trying to stream data through telematics into the cloud is going to need to use the broadband that is out there, the cell signal, or other things that could be put in place. Unless those are there, it is going to affect long-term the productivity and efficiency of our farms.

There has to be an effort, because we may not get the private investment because they are not sure of the payback. But once it is there in its entirety, because the problem is, if you just do a little area, you are not going to get it, but if it is there in its entirety, and that is where you need the government. I think that is where you create those private-public partnerships with the industry that is out there building telecommunications, because once it is all there the value to the United States is going to be tremendous.

I think that is what we have to understand. All this cloud that we talk about, it doesn't have any data unless we bring it from that dirt, the sensors stuck in the dirt, we have to get it there. And there is no technology to get it there, I mean, other than me capturing the data off it with a USB stick, going to it. But we will never implement those technologies, there has to be ease in the automation.

Mr. ROYSE. Sir, I would like to add that there are, as was mentioned, there are alternatives to broadband to capturing data, but they tend to be labor intensive, and we have one heck of a labor shortage out in California.

And we are not going to be able to use it, there is the labor shortage that broadband helps address. But also the fact that the more we can take humans out of the equation and make this more automated and more machine based, the more reliable the data is going to be. There are some ancillary concerns to this.

Ms. CASURELLA. What I will add to that is, right now it takes a technician to get the data. I will use an example of a farm in Illinois. It is all enabled with technology sensors, everything else, and the only time they are connected is when that tractor ends up back in the shed, they turn on their mobile device and stream that data. It is all after the fact.

And it is there, it is just really hard to get at, and again, takes a technician to figure out how to get the data anywhere, it is complicated, instead of letting the sensors talk to the cloud, which provides the information to the producer.

Mr. JANZEN. And I would add as well that it is not just a matter of some farmers in the United States not being connected and others being connected. We should always keep in mind that our farmers are operating in a global market and other countries are making these investments in rural broadband so their farmers have a competitive advantage. And we need to make sure that all of our farmers have that same advantage here when they put goods out on the world market.

Mr. LAWSON. I have little time left, but I wanted to say one thing. When you mentioned about California, about the labor shortage, are other countries experiencing the same kind of problem that California would be, experiencing a shortage of the labor market?

Mr. ROYSE. Are other countries experiencing? I don't know, but I do know that other countries, and we could talk a long time about what is going on in other countries. And we do a lot of work with China, India, and I was just recently in the Middle East, and they are in a race to implement technologies, including broadband, because they don't have the kind of agricultural infrastructure that the United States has. Other countries are becoming very automated very quickly.

Mr. LAWSON. Well, that is amazing.

Mr. Chairman, with that, I yield back.

The CHAIRMAN. The gentleman yields back.

I recognize the gentleman from Texas for 5 minutes.

Mr. DUNN. Thank you, Mr. Chairman.

And I echo the sentiments from my colleague, Mr. Lawson, there are just too many things happening at the same time. My apologies, especially if I repeat questions or comments that have already been made. I certainly want to thank all the panelists for being here and for your insight.

Utilizing data analytics, Billy, we talked about prior to this hearing, is a best practice across all industries. And I don't know that the ag industry, certainly ag producers, are fully utilizing those, and no telling what the gap is in terms of productivity and efficiency that we can gain.

But there is the question of who owns the data. You mentioned that. It is frustrating for you, why shouldn't the producer own that data.

What is government's role in being a data repository? I want the government in a very limited role. I want unleashing the market forces because that is where innovation happens. I don't think it happens a lot in the Federal Government. But the Federal Government has a role. Define that for me with respect to data.

Mr. TILLER. Well, I am going to keep it simple. The role has to remain in the private-sector of how we store the data, who owns it, because it is going to get too complex.

And I really think that most things work best when innovators innovate, and that is what has to happen. We can't have rules to make that happen.

But I am going to say that the role that could really be played is how we interact with land-grant universities, how we interact with research that is going on, and how that data could be used. I mean, farmers are in fear of that becoming FOIAble, and all they are trying to do is help in a research project.

That could be something you all could address, so that farmers could be part of a research project, help get to the real answers at the bottom, and not get in trouble just because they are trying to help others, because they might not even know they were wrong in what they have done.

I have heard stories out of California where somebody was plowing some ground and got into a multimillion dollar lawsuit or something, and it is all because he shared some data. That makes farmers fearful. They are like, I would rather not play at all.

The role has to be extremely limited. I think be very cautious. I would just caution, just like you said, just a little bit. We might need a little help and guidance.

And I don't have an answer how we bring that together. We just have to continue to innovate, encourage the producers to really work with groups like ours. If they want to digitally report like Deb's tool there, any way that you all could innovate that, there are cost savings to the government out of things like that.

Mr. DUNN. I can only imagine, as a bank board member, watching the burden and experiencing the burden of data collection that the government puts as a requirement because of deposit insurance and their regulatory role. I can appreciate why some would be very concerned about that, but someone has to have it.

And I agree with you, if you are going to innovate and you are going to manage effectively, the co-op idea, is really a brilliant idea. This is for other panelists, and, Billy, please weigh in if you have an idea on this, but, in my role at Texas Tech, trying to bring re- search to market, ideas, to transfer them to something that will make a difference in people's lives, this is the value proposition for R&D at the Federal Government. I am a big believer in it. It has made us competitive, more competitive than we would be otherwise without that investment.

But it is a very difficult endeavor to have early stage technology from government R&D to move through the process. You have to have the good idea that is patentable, marketable. You have to have capital, that is venture capital, angel investors, and other early stage money. And then you need to have entrepreneurs.

How do we make that a more efficient and a more successful proposition? Because taxpayers really get that. Some of this fundamental research, which I believe that basic science is important, too, but the applied and the transferred technology out of research, every taxpayer gets that, from Google to the Gatorade to all these things that have benefited us.

Tell me how we improve on that on this side of the ledger.

Mr. ROYSE. If I may offer a few comments.

Mr. DUNN. Please. Yes.

Then I am going to yield back, Mr. Chairman.

Mr. ROYSE. I know that Mr. Tiller doesn't like it when I use the word *disruptive,* but I will tell you that I have seen lots of very disruptive things. And just in business generally, that happens mostly at the startup level. I mean, big companies, publicly traded, they have shareholders to report to, they are not likely to swing for the fences like our small startup companies are, to come up with some really, truly game-changing technologies. Anything that encourages startup companies is good for innovation.

In my written comments I submitted a couple of proposals, I know it is not this Committee's purview, on some tax incentives that I think would go a long ways.

In terms of what the USDA can do, this trust issue is a real issue, it is a real thing between the tech companies and the farming community. And what is government's role? It should assume that traditional role of removing bad actors from the marketplace in order that we can have an atmosphere of a little more trust.

And we have a good model in the FTC Act. We just don't have an enforcement mechanism, that I am aware of, that applies to agriculture.

That is one thing that I think the Committee might want to consider.

The CHAIRMAN. The gentleman's time has expired.

And before we adjourn, I would like to recognize the Ranking Member for any closing comments he might have.

Mr. NOLAN. Thank you, Mr. Chairman.

I just want to thank the panel. It has been very revealing how important technology is for agriculture and the future of agriculture, and our ability to feed the world and to continue to grow and prosper. And I just want to thank each and every one of you.

And thank you, Mr. Chairman, for bringing in this really outstanding panel, we get a lot of panels here, but this is one of the really outstanding panels that we have had. And I commend to all of our colleagues and anybody interested in food and agricultural policy to take the opportunity to read through their testimony. It is just excellent. Thank you so much.

The CHAIRMAN. I thank my friend from Minnesota.

And I will close. I just want to share a few observations and thoughts real quick.

One of the recurring themes that we have heard, not only in this hearing, but in some listening sessions and prior hearings, was the need for broadband. And, obviously, that is going to continue to be a recurring theme.

Just thinking out loud here, we need to identify the key players from a technology standpoint, who can deliver and who can deliver and address changing technologies on the fly, first.

Second, who has the infrastructure to reach rural America, identify those.

And then, third, financing this. How do we do that? How big of a role, as you mentioned, how big of a role should the government play? Or should we be looking at public-private partnerships?

But I view this kind of like a three-legged stool. The technology is a big part of it. The infrastructure. Access, getting that technology delivered to the folks that need it. And then finally, the third piece of the pie here, the third leg of the three-legged stool, is financing. How do we pay for it? And that is going to be a struggle that we have to work toward collectively.

Big data, addressing any concerns, as we have talked about the privacy concerns, some of the skepticism that is inherent in agriculture, particularly where the government overlap takes place. The legal, ethical concerns, those privacy issues.

And then you mentioned this, Mr. Janzen, it is a marketable commodity, it really is. There is value in that data. How does the farmer realize the market potential to help improve his bottom line? There is definitely merit in exploring that and how you can monetize that data while protecting and safeguarding their privacy issues and things of that nature.

And then, finally, something that didn't come up, but just briefly, you may have touched on this, drone use, and how folks are using that and acquiring data through drones, how they are using this on their farms.

Folks are so innovative and creative out there. I have a group in my district that they are creating drones and different applications so fast that it is 4 months down the road this one becomes obsolete because they are advancing so quickly on the applications that they are finding for using unmanned aerial vehicles. And it becomes an issue with the FAA and FCC, potentially.

These are some things that we have to explore, and big data is the key and at the heart of that.

I just would associate myself with the comments that Mr. Nolan made. This is a great panel. And we begun a conversation here, but we didn't even scratch the surface on what the potential is for big data and how we can plug farmers into it in a more meaningful way.

Thank you for being here.

Under the Rules of the Committee, the record of today's hearing will remain open for 10 calendar days to receive additional material and supplementary written responses from the witnesses to any question posed by a Member.

This hearing of the Subcommittee on General Farm Commodities and Risk Management is adjourned.

[Whereupon, at 11:31 a.m., the Subcommittee was adjourned.]

www.ingramcontent.com/pod-product-compliance
Lightning Source LLC
Chambersburg PA
CBHW081121240526
45470CB00019B/2834